PENGUIN CLASSICS

THE ODES OF PINDAR

ADVISORY EDITOR: BETTY RADICE

Pindar was born in 518 B.C. near Thebes in Boiotia of an aristocratic family which sent him in boyhood to study music and poetry at Athens. When he was only twenty he was commissioned by the royal house of Thessaly to write *Pythian X*, and he soon found patrons in many parts of Greece and in Sicily, which he visited in 476. Pindar and the aristocratic families with whom he was at home in most parts of Greece, particularly in Aigina, were little interested in the new ideas which Athens was enforcing on Greek cities. When Pindar praised his own special world in 474 he was reprimanded and fined at Thebes. He realized how dangerous Athens was to his kind of society when, after 460, first Aigina, then Boiotia was conquered. Pindar reached the height of his fame and found the fullest scope of his powers in the seventies and sixties of the fifth century. He died at Argos *c.* 438. In antiquity his poems were collected in seventeen books, from which survive, more or less intact, four books of Epinician Odes – choral songs written in honour of victories in the great Games.

Sir Maurice Bowra studied Greek at Oxford under Gilbert Murray and gained first class honours. In 1922 he became tutor and fellow of Wadham College, Oxford, and in 1938 he was made Warden, a post which he retained until his death in 1971. From 1946 to 1950 he was Professor of Poetry in the University, and from 1951 to 1954 he was its Vice-Chancellor. From 1958 to 1962 he was President of the British Academy. He wrote a number of books on Greek subjects, but also extended his studies to include parts of other literatures. He travelled a great deal in Greece, Asia Minor, and the Near East, and the United States. He was knighted in 1951, became a Commander of the Legion of Honour, a Doctor of Letters of Oxford University, and was the holder of eight honorary doctorates.

The Odes of Pindar

translated with an introduction by
C. M. BOWRA

PENGUIN BOOKS

PENGUIN BOOKS

Published by the Penguin Group
Penguin Books Ltd, 27 Wrights Lane, London W8 5TZ, England
Penguin Putnam Inc., 375 Hudson Street, New York, New York 10014, USA
Penguin Books Australia Ltd, Ringwood, Victoria, Australia
Penguin Books Canada Ltd, 10 Alcorn Avenue, Toronto, Ontario, Canada M4V 3B2
Penguin Books (NZ) Ltd, Private Bag 102902, NSMC, Auckland, New Zealand

Penguin Books Ltd, Registered Offices: Harmondsworth, Middlesex, England

This collection first published 1969

Printed in England by Clays Ltd, St Ives plc
Set in Monotype Bembo

CONTENTS

CONTENTS

PREFACE

IN 1928 Professor H. T. Wade-Gery and I published with the Nonesuch Press a little book, *Pindar: Pythian Odes*. This contained translations of all the Pythian Odes, together with a general introduction and separate introductions to the individual poems. The book, which was charmingly produced, very soon sold out and has not been reprinted. After forty years I have gone back to it and tried to make it the core of a complete translation of Pindar's Epinician Odes. The Nonesuch Press has given permission for it to be reproduced in this way, and though Professor Wade-Gery has not been able to collaborate in new translations, he has willingly given permission for the republication of the Pythian Odes, in all of which he had a large share. So the Pythian Odes are here printed, with very few and small exceptions, as they were in 1928. The others are my own work, made over a period of years. Considerations of space have discouraged me from reprinting the original introductions, but as Pindar is notoriously difficult to understand, I have added a few notes of explanation to each poem. I am not convinced that they are adequate, but I hope that they will give some help. I have also added at the end of the book a register of names to assist in deciphering Pindar's allusive methods of nomenclature. I have confined myself to the complete odes and not made any attempt to translate the fragments. I have arranged the poems in what seems to me a likely chronological order, as this may help to illustrate Pindar's development, but I am conscious that much in it is uncertain. I have followed the text of my own *Pindari Carmina* in the Oxford Classical Texts, and in the very few places where I have diverged from it, I record the fact in a note.

In my translation I have followed the method of the earlier book and made no attempt to keep either Pindar's metres, which cannot be reproduced in English, or his formality of structure. I have tried to maintain a kind of free verse, but I have aimed much more at preserving the meaning of the original than its rhythm. I have not made my lines correspond with Pindar's, and the numbers in the margin refer to the Greek original and not to the English translation. I have put them in since, even with this defect, I hope that they will make it easier to look up references.

I owe a great debt to Father Peter Levi, s.j., who has read my text with generous care and made many wise suggestions. For the many faults that remain I must myself bear the responsibility.

C.M.B.

INTRODUCTION

I

PINDAR was born in 518 B.C. near Thebes in Boiotia. His family was aristocratic and claimed connexion with the ancient clan of the Aigeidai, which was important at Sparta and through its branch at Thera numbered the royal house of Kyrene among its members. Pindar's family did not merit the common Greek gibe that the Boiotians were ignorant boors, for they sent him in boyhood to study music and poetry at Athens. The last tyrant had just been expelled and a radically new democracy was being created, but though later in life Pindar was to be alarmed and even horrified by the unprecedented policies of Athens, he can hardly have foreseen them at this time. What he must have studied was the art of the choral ode, which had won a special prominence at Athens in the annual competitions for Dithyrambs in honour of Dionysos. In these Simonides, from the neighbouring island of Keos, won a long succession of prizes, and the fragments of his work show certain similarities to Pindar's. Pindar matured rapidly. When he was only twenty he was commissioned by the royal house of Thessaly to write *Pythian X*, which is already highly accomplished and forecasts much that is most characteristic in Pindar's later work. Before long he found patrons in many parts of Greece and in Sicily, and formed connexions, which meant much to him for the rest of his life, with noble families in Aigina. He seems hardly to have noticed the first wave of Persian invasion in 490 B.C., which ended in defeat by the Athenians at Marathon, but when the Persians returned with a more formidable army and fleet in 480-479 B.C., he was caught in an ugly position; for, while his friends in Aigina took a leading part in the defeat of the Persian fleet at Salamis, his own Thebes fought on the Persian side and earned the deadly hatred of those other Greeks who opposed it.

Pindar's anguished feelings are revealed in *Isthmian VIII*, but the general dislike of Thebes does not seem to have included him, nor is there any sign that he wished the Persians to win. Almost before the war was finished he was writing for Aiginetan friends, and soon afterwards he was invited by generous and powerful patrons elsewhere to celebrate their successes. In Sicily Hieron of Syracuse and Theron of Akragas were military autocrats who wished to enhance their reputations on the Greek mainland and were rich enough to make a fine showing in the great Games in which victory was prized beyond all other honours. When in 476 B.C. Hieron won the horse-race and Theron the chariot-race in the Olympian Games, Pindar accepted an invitation to visit Sicily and supervise the performance of his own odes in honour of the victories. He stayed for the winter, but returned to the mainland in the spring and never visited Sicily again. From *Pythian II* we form the impression that he was not happy in a tyrant's court and preferred to compose poems for his Sicilian patrons in the detachment of his own home.

Pindar reached the height of his fame and found the fullest scope of his powers in the seventies and sixties of the fifth century. Though Thebes was his native place and, despite intermittent conflicts, he kept a loyal affection for it, he was at home among aristocratic families in almost any part of Greece. If Aigina won his deepest love, he entered easily into the spirit of successful athletes in Rhodes, Argos, and Korinth, and above all gave of his fullest powers to Arkesilas IV, king of Kyrene, for whom he wrote on an almost epic scale his *Pythian IV*. The families which he favoured and which favoured him belonged to an old-fashioned world and were little interested in the new ideas which Athens was enforcing on Greek cities. Even if they survived, it must have been at

some cost to themselves in vitality and creative vigour. Nor
did they all survive. The military monarchies of Theron and
Hieron collapsed after their deaths; Arkesilas was murdered
by his own people soon after the performance of *Pythian IV*.
Pindar was slow to see that Athens threatened his own special
world, and about 474 B.C. praised it in some famous words:

> O glittering, violet-crowned, chanted in song,
> Bulwark of Hellas, renowned Athens,
> Citadel of the Gods.

For this he was reprimanded and fined at Thebes, and traces
of the dispute and his own defence can be seen in *Pythian IX*.
For a time he failed or refused to see how dangerous Athens
was to the kind of society which meant everything to him,
but after 460 B.C. he saw the brutal truth when Athens con-
quered first Aigina and later Boiotia. His later poems sym-
bolized Athens variously as the arrogant Bellerophon, the
murderous Aigisthos, and the unruly giant Porphyrion. His
latest extant poem, *Pythian VIII*, written in 446 B.C., recog-
nizes and approves the desire of Aigina to be free of Athens
in what looks like a very favourable moment, but even so
Pindar has doubts and misgivings and sees the passing issues
of politics in a much wider setting.

Pindar died at Argos *c.* 438 B.C., not long before the out-
break of the Peloponnesian War, but he had lived to see the
liberation of Boiotia at the battle of Koroneia in 447 B.C. But
though he could not fail to be touched by political events,
especially when they affected his friends, Pindar saw human
affairs from a more exalted and more exalting level. He
belonged to an older world than we associate with the fifth
century, its Athenian innovations and restless energy and
pursuit of power. He admired heroism, but had no great
liking for war, and preferred that things should stay as they
were and men cultivate peace with one another and with

themselves. He lived through one of the most eventful periods of history, but hardly marked its salient characteristics. He was concerned with the individuals whom he knew and with the world of gods above and around them that made them what they were.

2

In antiquity Pindar's poems were collected in seventeen books. From these survive, more or less intact, four books of Epinician Odes, that is choral songs written in honour of victories in the great Games. Though many cities of Greece held games, the most highly regarded were the Olympian, held at Olympia in Elis, and the Pythian, held at Delphoi, both in every fourth year, and the Nemean, held in the north-east Peloponnese, and the Isthmian, held on the Isthmos of Korinth, both in every second year. Each of the four books of Epinicians deals with one of these Games. Of Pindar's other books we have many fragments but no complete poem of any size. We might think it an odd whim of chance to have preserved the Epinicians when so little remains of such promising material as Hymns, Dirges, and Dithyrambs. But in fact, though the survival of the Epinicians may be largely an accident, there is no reason to complain; for in them Pindar deals with a great deal more than athletic success. So far as the actual Games were concerned, he seems to have been not very interested in their details; what concerned him was the significance of success in his scheme of things. For him victory in the Games raised questions of mystical and metaphysical importance. It illustrated the fact of glory as something which came from the Gods and the reality of success which is won by a proper use of natural gifts and laborious effort. The result is that the Epinicians contain a mass of poetry about many matters which range from a vision of life after death to many lively and stirring accounts of mythical events. It is hard to think of any subject which Pindar would normally have put into some other kind of poem and does not bring sooner or later into an Epinician. One advantage of his comparative lack of interest in the actual Games was that he found himself moved to speak of many other, more exalted matters and to use some actual occasion to convey his inner convictions.

3

The Epinician Ode is extremely formal in structure and governed by strict rules. In its simpler form, as in *Pythian VI* or *Nemean VIII*, it consists of a series of strophes or stanzas, each of which is metrically identical with all the rest, and this identity extends even to small points of prosody. Alternatively, and more often, Pindar uses not a series of single, similar strophes, but a series of triads, each of which consists of strophe, antistrophe, and epode, or, as Ben Jonson called them, Turne, Counter-Turne, and Stand. Strophe and antistrophe are metrically identical not merely in the same triad but throughout the poem, and though the epode is different from them, all epodes in a single poem are exactly alike. This is a very demanding structure, and its demands are seen more clearly when we find that no poem of Pindar is metrically the same as any other. Each time that he composed a poem he invented a new metrical pattern. It is true that his patterns are based on recognizable principles and that rhythmically his odes may be divided roughly into two classes, which may be called Dorian and Aeolian, but each single poem has its own metrical individuality. It is impossible to reproduce Pindar's metres in English, and even in Greek, where the quantitative system allows so much more variety and assurance than our own accentual system, it takes a little time to catch their lilt and movement, but once it is caught it has no rival in variety, speed, and lightness.

Yet Pindar's formality is almost entirely external. It does not correspond to anything in what he has to say. Sometimes he ends a theme or a sentence with the end of a triad, but more often he sails gaily beyond it. Moreover, he does not present his material in an obviously formal arrangement but often seems to enjoy puzzling his readers by following some whimsical, apparently unmeditated plan. He is not interested in making an obvious beginning, middle, and end, but places his ingredients as his fancy wills. Though he learned his craft in Athens, it was in origin Dorian, and we can trace its history back to at least the seventh century. From a very early date the choral ode, such as the Epinician was, contained diverse elements sanctioned by tradition which the poet was expected to bring together. He had to praise the gods, to tell something about his human subject and his family, to illustrate the present occasion by a myth drawn from legend, and to enunciate grave truths in the form of maxims. All these things Pindar does but in no given order and with no recurring rules or proportion. More than this, his method of progression is more often than not by apparently abrupt changes of subject, which leave us guessing what his intention is. These changes are usually clear if we look closely at them, but Pindar likes to surprise us by the way in which he manages them. These traditional elements he understands intimately, and his control of them indicates how ancient they are and how welcome is variety in their treatment. But both the divergent character of his main elements and his handling of them make him a difficult author.

No formula solves the difficulty of reading Pindar, but it becomes less formidable when we remember that in each poem he is writing for a single occasion and that the main elements in this complex whole must somehow have a place in his poem. As he moves from theme to theme, from particular to general, from meditative wisdom to exciting narrative, he adds something new to his whole effect which is never fully visible until the whole pattern has been displayed. Even when he tells a myth it is not at all in the straightforward Homeric manner. He assumes that his audience know the main outline of his myths, and from his material he selects the points that appeal most strongly to him and enriches them with his finest poetry, but though his high moments can be intensely dramatic, his method is often whimsical and ingenious. He leads us through a series of different effects – narrative, personal, didactic – and we find ourselves shifting from one mood to another as he imposes his enchantment on us. Once we grasp his method and follow its twists and turns through a poem we see how rich his understanding of a single occasion is, how much new matter he finds in it and how much he gives to it.

4

Pindar's style, like that of most Greek poetry, is a highly artificial creation with roots in a distant past. Greece had no single, common speech but every district had its own dialect. Sometimes a local dialect was used for poetry, but then its popularity was necessarily limited, as it might not be intelligible in some other places. Just as the epic was composed in a language which everyone understood because he was brought up on it, and contained a large variety of forms and synonyms, so did the language of choral song. It had a Dorian colouring, as the epic had an Ionian, but it was not any spoken Dorian dialect. It had been built up for some three centuries, and in the course of time had developed not only a rich vocabulary with many linguistic variations but a large number of literary devices. Pindar's allusive methods and indirect progress gain much from little tricks which give surprise and variety to his movement. Above all he secures a remarkable concentration in his use of words. He is able by judicious omission and selection to say a lot in a very small space – not in the sense that he conveys much information, but in the sense that the poetical weight and force of a phrase or a sentence are much more noticeable than in more straight-forward poetical speech. This kind of concentration sometimes comes at the end of a long tradition, and though it may always have been natural to Greek choral song, it is understandable that Pindar, writing in his own way in an ancient form, secures an even greater richness than his predecessors, and if we may judge by the fragments of poets like Simonides or Pindar's own contemporary Bacchylides, this is what he does. Pindar comes at the end of a long tradition, and sums up in himself the special outlook of the aristocratic age of Greece.

5

Pindar's guiding and central theme is the part of experience in which human beings are exalted or illumined by a divine force, and this he commonly compares with light. At such times the consciousness is marvellously enhanced, and a man's whole being has a new spaciousness and confidence. For Pindar this was the end and the justification of life, and he regarded himself as almost uniquely qualified to provide it. He has few words of praise for other poets and sees himself as supremely endowed by nature and training for his special task. Through song men attain immortality, even though this is not easily defined and seems to depend on being remembered by later generations. What Pindar conveys in song is precisely the enhancement of consciousness which his athletes enjoy in the moment of triumph. This is the central inspiration of Pindar's work and accounts for his special quality. His vision is of a world in which both men and gods are active but all that really matters comes directly from the

gods. For much of their time men lead a shadowy and un-
substantial existence, but when the gods send a divine bright-
ness all is well with them. It is this brightness that Pindar
seeks to convey. Even in his myths, where there are many
vivid and stirring moments, there is very little pathos, still
less tragic tension. What Pindar catches is the joy beyond
ordinary emotions as it transcends and transforms them. It
can be found in athletic success, convivial relaxation, song and
music, friendship and love, in many natural sights and sounds,
in prayer and hymns. He is a religious poet. He knows that
everything worth having comes from the gods, that they are
everywhere, that in any analysis men are as nothing compared
with them, but just for this reason the poet's task is to catch
and keep the fleeting divine moment and to reveal to men
what really matters in their busy bustling lives. Because he
believes this, Pindar stands above politics and seeks his own
eternal ends wherever they are to be found. It may be true
that his art looks not forward but backward, that the past
holds him and the future interests him not at all, but that is
to say very little. He embodies with a notable purity certain
spiritual forces which inspired and sustained the Greeks in
their heyday and were by no means without honour even in
Athens.

In antiquity Pindar's poetry was thought to suffer from
extraordinary lapses, and no doubt it does. It must have been
difficult for him to rise with an authentic splendour to lists of
athletic victories or genealogical details. His special vision
could not possibly be at work with equal power everywhere,
and we must remember that he was a professional poet who
was invited to write on themes not of his own choosing, and
almost certainly paid for doing so. He believed absolutely in
the need of inspiration; he knew what it was and made the
most of it. He also knew that even the most inspired poet
must also be a craftsman who takes trouble with his craft.

This too he did, and even when he does not thrill us he may charm us by his inventive ingenuity in handling some intractable topic. Yet so many and so sustained are his fine flights that we can understand that the Greeks compared him with an eagle and thought him their greatest lyric poet. This was what he too believed, and we may agree with him.

Chariot-race

The chariots were four-horsed. The course was twelve double laps, nearly nine miles. Accidents were frequent. When Arkesilas IV, king of Kyrene, sent a chariot to compete at the Pythian Games in 462 B.C., it survived when forty crashed.

Mule-car race

This was introduced at Olympia early in the fifth century B.C. but discontinued in 444 B.C.

Horse-race

The course was one lap of six stades, about 1,200 yards. The jockeys rode without saddles or stirrups.

Foot-race

This was from one end of the stadium to the other, about 200 yards.

Double foot-race

This was from one end of the stadium to the other, and then back, in all about 400 yards.

Long foot-race

This varied at different places, but at Olympia was about three miles.

Race in armour

This was introduced towards the end of the sixth century.

The runner wore at least a helmet and carried a shield on his left arm.

Wrestling

The normal aim was to throw your opponent on the ground. A fall on the back or shoulders or hip counted as a fair throw. Three clean throws were needed for victory.

Boxing

There were no regular rounds, and no confined ring. The fight was to the finish, with either a knock-out or an admission of defeat. There was no rule against hitting a man when down. Thongs tied round the hands and wrists took the place of gloves.

Five Events

The *pentathlon* was a combined competition in running, jumping (long jump only), throwing the discus, throwing the javelin, and wrestling.

Trial of strength

The *pankration* was a competition in boxing and wrestling combined with kicking, strangling, and twisting. Biting and gouging were forbidden, but most other manoeuvres were not. You might kick your opponent in the belly, twist his foot out of its socket, or break his fingers. All neck-holds were allowed, a favourite being the 'ladder-grip' in which you climbed your opponent's back, wound your legs round his belly, and your arms round his neck.

Flute

Early competitions in the Pythian Games seem often to have been musical, but in the fifth century that in flute-playing alone survived.

PYTHIAN X

*For Hippokleas of Thessaly, winner in the boys'
double foot-race*

I

Happy Lakedaimon,
Blessed Thessaly! in both
One father begot their race of kings,
Herakles bravest in battle.
    What are these high untimely words?
Pytho, and the town of Pelinna, call to me
And the sons of Aleuas call, that I should bring
5 In triumph
For Hippokleas the loud voice of men.

He is tasting the Games.
To the host of the dwellers around
That vale in Parnassos
Proclaimed him, first of the boys
In the double foot-race.
10   Apollo, sweet is the end of endeavour
(Sweet too its beginning)
When a God speeds its growing.
I think you planned that he should win this;
And the blood in him follows his father's tracks,

Who won at Olympia twice
 In the armour of Ares which takes the shock of war;
15 And the Games under the rocks of Krisa,
In that deep meadow, put
Phrikias first in the runners' race.
May their luck hold, and keep in the days to come
Their lordly wealth aflower!

II

So great a share of the lovely things of Hellas
Is theirs, let God not envy them
And change their fortune.
  Though God alone never tastes woe,
Yet that man is happy and poets sing of him,
Who conquers with hand or swift foot
And wins the greatest of prizes
By steadfastness and strength

And lives to see
His young son, in turn, get garlands at Pytho.
He shall never climb the brazen sky;
But what glittering things we mortal men attain,
He travels there
To the farthest edge of sailing.
But not in ships or on foot
Will you find the marvellous road
To the games of the People beyond the North.

Perseus the prince has been at their feasts.
He came to their houses
And found them making high sacrifice
Of a hundred asses to their God.
In their feasts for ever and their praises
Is Apollo's chief delight;
He laughs as he sees
Their beasts' high-cocked presumption!

III

And the Muse never leaves that land,
For this is their life:
Everywhere the girls are dancing,
And the sound of the harps is loud,

And the noise of the flutes.
40 They bind their hair with bay leaves of gold,
They feast and are glad.
And sickness never, nor cursed old age
Touches their holy bodies:
Without toil, without war

They dwell, and do not trouble
The stern scales of Nemesis.
Breathing the courage of his heart
45 Came Danaä's son,
Athana his guide,
To visit the Fortunate Ones.
He slew the Gorgon
And came with that head of writhing serpent-hair
To the islanders, and struck them
Dead in stone.
        But for me no wonder

50 If the Gods do it, nor anything hard for belief.
Easy the oar: drop the anchor quick from the bows.
Let it bite the bottom, to keep us off the reef.
The light of the holiday-song
Darts from one thought to another like a bee!

IV

55 I hope that when men of Ephyra
Pour out sweet music beside Peneios
They will make Hippokleas with their singing
More splendid than ever,
For the wreathes he has won,
Among his fellows and elders,
And the young girls will look at him.
60 – For many loves trouble the hopes of men.

23

To each his heart's desire:
And when he gets it,
Ravishingly sweet will he find
The common thoughts he comes by;
And there's no guessing
What any twelvemonth brings.
I know this:
Thorax is busy with delights for his friends!
Who for my sake took pains to harness
65 This four-horse chariot of the Muses.
He loves me, I him: he my guide, I his, in friendship.

At the test, gold is proved by the touchstone,
And so is a true mind.
I have praise yet
For his excellent brothers, who bear on high
70 The Thessalians' land
And bring it to power.
   In the hands of good men lies
The noble piloting of cities
Handed from father to son.

Pythian X was composed in 498 B.C., when Pindar was twenty years old. It was performed at the Thessalian town of Pelinna, not far from Larisa, the seat of the princely house of the Aleuads, with whom the victor was connected. Pindar himself was present. The real host and patron was Thorax, who was *tagos* or chief prince of Thessaly.

1–3 The association between Thessaly and Sparta through the common descent of their respective royal houses from Herakles reflects the present attempts of Sparta, under its king, Kleomenes, to extend Spartan power over northern Greece by a system of alliances.

15–16 The father of Hippokleas, Phrikias, has twice won the foot-race in armour at Olympia and once at Delphoi. The 'rocks of Krisa' are the rocky slopes of Parnassos, in whose flank the stadium at Delphoi was cut above the temple and the theatre.

29–49 Pindar tells of the fabulous Hyperboreans or People beyond the North, of whom there was some cult in Thessaly. He combines them with Perseus, who was also connected with Thessaly and visited the Hyperboreans in his quest for the Gorgon. The point of the myth is that the Hyperboreans are ideally happy, and that though no mere men can enjoy a like happiness, Hippokleas and his friends come as near as possible to it.

44 Perseus, son of Danaä, kills the Gorgon Medoisa and with her head turns into stone the people of the island of Seriphos. See *Pythian XII*, 12.

69 Thorax is assisted in the government of Thessaly by his brothers Eurypylos and Thrasydaios.

PYTHIAN VI

For Xenokrates of Akragas, winner in the chariot-race

I

Listen! it is Aphrodite of the sudden glances,
Or is it the Graces, whose field we are ploughing now
On our road to the thunderous Earth's enshrinèd navel,
Where, for a Pythian conqueror, waits
5 A treasure-house of songs,
For the happy Emmenidai, for Akragas on her river,
And for Xenokrates: it is built with walls
In Apollo's gold-stored combe.

II

10 No wintry storms driving over,
Nor the loud thundercloud's
Merciless army, nor the gale,
Shall sweep it, pounded in devouring silt,
Into the gulfs of the sea.
Its porch, in the pure light,
Shall stand, the herald of a conquest
That a chariot won in the fold of Krisa Hill,
Glorious in the mouths of men,
15 Your father's, Thrasyboulos, and all your clan's.

III

You keep him on your right hand,
20 Not swerving from the commandment:
Among the mountains, they say, Philyra's son
Gave to the mighty child of Peleus far away from his
     home

This counsel: 'Zeus Kronidas,
The deep-voiced Lord of Lightning and Thunderbolts,
Him thou shalt worship first of Gods:
25 And a like honour
Give to thy parents for the length of their days.'

IV

Antilochos was a warrior long ago
Who kept this purpose.
30 For he died for his father,
Braving the murderous
Memnon, prince of the Ethiopian host.
– Nestor's chariot was held
(An arrow of Paris pierced his horse): and Memnon
Came on with mighty spear.
35 And the old Messenian, shaken at heart,
Cried upon his son.

V

That cry cast forth
Did not fall to the ground.
There he stood fast, a more than man,
And paid his death for the rescue of his father:
40 And gained, through his tremendous deed,
Among younger generations,
This fame, that he of the men of old
Was best son to his father.
   It was long ago:
Of men now, Thrasyboulos has come nearest
45 To what a father would have,

VI

And follows in all
His uncle's paths of splendour.

He gives thought to his wealth,
Not plucking in violence or wrong
The flower of youth, but of wisdom
In the secret places of Pieria's Maids.
50 You, Earth-Shaker, master of running horses,
He pleases greatly, Poseidon: his thoughts are of you.
Sweet is his heart,
And when his companions feast with him, is like
Those cells the bees brim full.

Pythian VI was composed in 490 B.C. and performed at Delphoi soon
after the victory, Pindar himself being present. Xenokrates was the
brother of the Sicilian Theron, tyrant of Akragas, and a man of con-
siderable consequence, but Pindar is more interested in his young son
Thrasyboulos.

8–18 The song is compared with one of the treasuries built on the slope
of Delphoi (the Athenian Treasury has been reconstructed from its
original stones), and, like them, will defy all storms.

18 The chariot-race in the Pythian Games took place in the valley
below Parnassos.

22 Philyra's son is the Centaur Cheiron, who was the tutor of some
great heroes. A lost work, The *Precepts of Cheiron*, seems to have con-
tained apophthegms like that quoted by Pindar here.

28–39 Antilochos saved his father Nestor at the cost of his own life, and
is held up to Thrasyboulos as a model son.

53 There survive a few lines from a drinking-song composed by Pindar
for Thrasyboulos and presumably sung after the supper for the victory:

Thrasyboulos, this chariot of love-songs
I send to you after supper. May it be shared by all
Among the drinkers and Dionysos' fruits

And the cups from Athens, a stinging delight;
When the wearying cares of men pass away
From their breasts, and in the sea of golden wealth

All alike we sail to a shore of lies.
When he who has nothing is rich, and in turn the wealthy ...

PYTHIAN XII

For Midas of Akragas, winner in the flute-playing

I

I pray you, lover of splendour, fairest of mortal cities,
Persephona's home,
Queen, dwelling on your well-built height, where below
On the banks of Akragas the sheep are grazing,
5 Take this Pythian wreath
Achieved by glorious Midas, and take himself,
Victor of Hellas
In that art which Pallas Athana invented, when
She wove to a tune
The ruthless Gorgon's deathly dirge;

II

Which Perseus heard, pouring from those Virgins' lips
10 And the unapproachable serpent-heads,
In that woeful struggle, when he destroyed
The third part of the Sisters;
And brought to Seriphos in the sea
Her people's doom and her own.
Ay, and he darkened the unearthly brood
Of Phorkos and made Polydektas rue
The gifts he asked for, and Danaä's
15 Long slavery and forced love!
For he had as his spoil broad-cheeked Medoisa's head,

III

The son of Danaä: who, I say,
Was conceived of the living gold.

And when she delivered from these labours
The man she loved, the Maiden created
The flute's wide-ranging music, to copy in it
That strong and loud lamentation
20 Which reached her from Euryala's eager jaws.
The Goddess invented it, and gave her invention
To mortal men,
Naming it 'The Many-Headed Tune',
The glorious summons
To the multitudinous games,

IV

25 Blown through thin bronze, and blown through the reeds
Which grow near the fair-spaced city of the Graces
In the garden of the Nymph of Kaphisos.
Wherever dancing is, they are sure to be.
    Any bliss that man may win
(And without labour, none!) God shall perfect
Today, perhaps! but fate may not be escaped.
Then lo! Time's hand,
Throwing at you the unforeseen
Turns calculation upside down, and gives you
One thing, but another not yet.

Pythian XII, like *Pythian VI*, was composed in 490 B.C. Midas had prob-
ably come in the entourage of Xenokrates. It was probably meant to be
performed on his return to Akragas, when Pindar would not be present.

1–3 Pindar had not yet visited Akragas and describes it from hearsay,
quite correctly.

6–17 Athana invented the flute, and also a tune called 'The Many-
Headed', which was supposed to be the lament of the Gorgon Euryala
for her sister Medoisa, when Perseus killed her.

11 Perseus kills only Medoisa, and leaves the other two Gorgons alive.

12 He turns the inhabitants of Seriphos, with their king Polydektas,
into stone for their maltreatment of his mother Danaä.

14 The Gorgons are children of Phorkos, but so are the Graiai, who had only one eye and one tooth between them. Perseus took the eye to force them to tell him where the Gorgons lived, and when they did, omitted to give it back to them.

17 Perseus was conceived when Zeus came to Danaä in a shower of gold.

26 The Graces were worshipped in Orchomenos. See *Olympian XIV*.

28–32 The ancient commentators say that Midas' flute broke during his performance, but that he continued to play without a mouth-piece.

OLYMPIAN XIV

For Asopichos of Orchomenos, winner in the foot-race

I

The waters of Kaphisos belong
To the place of fine horses where you dwell,
Queens of song, in sparkling Orchomenos,
Graces, who watch
Over the ancient race of the Minyans,
5 Hear, when I pray. By your help
All sweet and delightful things
Belong to men; if anyone
Is wise or lovely or famous.
For without the holy Graces
Not even the Gods rule dances or feasts.
10 They dispose all that is done in Heaven;
Their thrones are set
At the side of Pythian Apollo, the golden-bowed,
And they worship the everlasting glory
Of the Father on Olympos.

II

O Lady Glory, and Mirth, delighting in music,
Children of the most mighty of Gods,
15 Listen now, and Health, lover of the dance,
Look on the company lightly treading after friendly
fortune.
I have come with a song for Asopichos
In the Lydian style with careful art;
For through you the Minyan race

20 Is victorious at Olympia.
    Go now, Echo, to the black walls
Of Persephona's house
And bring the fine news to his father;
See Kleodamos and tell him
How his son
In the famous valleys of Pytho
Has crowned his young hair
With the wings of a glorious triumph.

Olympian XIV was probably composed in 488 B.C. to be sung on the victor's return to his native Orchomenos, where the Graces – Aglaia (Glory), Euphrosyna (Mirth), and Thalia (Health) – had a prominent place in local cult.

4 Minyas was the legendary founder of Orchomenos; hence its inhabitants are Minyans.

20 ff. The victor's father, Kleodamos, has recently died, but Pindar assumes that he is able to hear of his son's success.

PYTHIAN VII

For Megakles of Athens, winner in the chariot-race

Athens the mighty city!
For the strong house of the Alkmaionidai
This is the finest prelude
To lay as foundation-stone
Of my chariot-song.
For in what country, what clan, would you dwell
5 And have more magnificent renown
For Hellas to hear?

For in every city the story runs
Of the citizens of Erechtheus,
Who built in shining Pytho
Thy porch, Apollo, marvellous to behold.
10 There call to me also
Five victories at the Isthmos
And one paramount at God's Olympia
And two by Krisa,

Megakles, yours and your fathers'!
And in this last happy fortune
Some pleasure I have; but sorrow as well
15 At envy requiting your fine deeds.
– Thus always, they say,
Happiness, flowering and constant,
Brings after it
One thing with another.

Pythian VII was composed in 486 B.C. and performed at Delphoi after
the victory, Pindar himself being present. Megakles was a leading
Athenian statesman who had been ostracized from Athens early in the
same year. He was recalled before the Persian invasion of 480 B.C.

9 The Alkmaionid clan, to which Megakles belonged, had built a new marble portico for the temple of Apollo at Delphoi. The temple of which ruins now survive dates from the fourth century, but small pieces of the Alkmaionid portico have been found.

15 Envy is seen as the reason for Megakles' ostracism. It was probably due to his opposition to the policies of Themistokles.

NEMEAN II

For Timodamos of Acharnai, winner in the
trial of strength

I

Just as the sons of Homer,
Singers of interwoven lines,
Often begin with a prelude to Zeus,
So this man also
Has taken the first instalment of victory
In the holy Games
5 In the far-sung wood of Nemean Zeus.

II

Needs must be henceforward
That if the life which guides him straight
On his father's road
Has given glory to mighty Athens,
Timonoos' son shall often reap
The finest harvest of victories
10 At the Isthmos and in the Pythian Games. It is right

III

That Orion should travel
Not far from the Doves of the mountains.
Truly Salamis has strength
To breed a man for the fight.
In Troy Hektor heard of Aias.
Timodamos, your stout-hearted valour
15 In the Trial of Strength gives you increase.

36

IV

In old tales Acharnai
Had brave men, and in every event of the Games
The sons of Timodamos
Are proclaimed for excelling.
By Parnassos, monarch on high,
They brought home four victories in the struggles,
20 But from men of Korinth

V

In the valleys of high-born Pelops
They have already had eight wreaths fastened on them,
And seven at Nemea – and at home
Past counting – in the Games of Zeus.
    Of him, townsmen, sing in your revel
When Timodamos comes home in glory,
25 And lead on with the sweet-toned voice.

Nemean II was composed about 485 B.C. The victor comes from
Acharnai in Attica.

1–3 The Sons of Homer were a guild of professional rhapsodes, whose
chief task was to recite the Homeric poems, to which they made pro-
prietary claims. The 'interwoven lines' may mean that one rhapsode
would take over from another and so ensure a succession of reciters.
Sometimes a Son of Homer would, before getting to his main task,
recite a poem to some god, such as Zeus, and this is what Pindar has in
mind here. Such hymns were called 'preludes'.

10–12 When Orion pursued the Doves, they were saved by being
turned into the constellation of the Pleiads. Pindar makes a play on
words between 'Orion' and 'mountains', and his point is that after
some minor victories Timodamos should win a great one.

13 Presumably the victor has also some connexion with Salamis, the
home of Aias.

NEMEAN V

For Pytheas of Aigina, winner in the trial of strength

I

I am no maker of statues
Who fashions figures to stand unmoved
On the self-same pedestal.
On every merchantman, in every skiff
Go, sweet song, from Aigina,
And spread the news that Lampon's son,
Pytheas, sturdy and strong,
Has won the wreath for All Strength in the Nemean
    Games,
5 Though his cheeks show not yet the summer,
Mother of the grape's soft down.

To hero-spearmen sprung from Kronos and Zeus
And from the golden Nereids,
To the Aiakidai, he has brought honour
And to his mother-city, land that loves strangers.
    Of old they made her
Noble in men and renowned in ships,
10 When they stood by the altar of Father Hellanios
And together spread out their hands to the sky,
The glorious sons of Endaïs,
With Phokos, the mighty prince,

Child of a goddess; – him the Sand-maiden
Bore where the sea-waves were breaking.
I am shy of speaking of a huge risk
Unrightfully hazarded,
How they left the fair-famed island,

15 And what fate drove brave men from the Vineland.
I shall halt. Truth does not always
Gain if she displays
Her face unflinching;
And silence is often a man's wisest counsel.

II

If my purpose is set to praise
Wealth or strength of hands or iron-clad war,
20 Dig a long pit for my jump from here;
I have a light spring in my knees.
Eagles swoop even across the sea.
– For those men also graciously
The loveliest choir of Muses sang
On Pelion, and in their midst
Apollo swept the seven-tongued harp
With a golden quill

25 And led songs in every kind.
They began with Zeus
And sang first of holy Thetis and Peleus,
– How the luxurious daughter of Kretheus,
Hippolyta, wished to snare him by a trick;
By elaborate craft she had won the help
Of her lord who watched over the Magnesians.
She rigged a false, lying tale
That Peleus tried to sleep with her,
30 The bride of Akastos,
In his marriage-bed.

The truth was the opposite.
For often she tried to beguile him
And begged him with all her heart.
Her steep words stung him to anger,
And forthwith he scorned her embraces –

39

He was afraid of his Father's anger, the God of Guests.
35 But cloud-mover Zeus, King of Immortals,
Marked well and promised from the sky that soon
He should have for wife
A sea-maiden from the golden-spindled Nereids,

III

And win over their kinsman Poseidon.
– Often he comes from Aigai
To the famous Dorian Isthmos.
There the glad companies greet him, a God,
40 With the peal of pipes and the rivalry of bold strong
        limbs.
    The fate born with a man gives the verdict
On all that he does. You, Euthymenes,
Have fallen twice from Aigina into Victory's arms
And clasped elaborate songs.

And now you also, Pytheas,
Have sprung after him,
And your mother's brother exalts you,
A scion of the same stock as Peleus.
Nemea is tied to you,
And the month of this land which Apollo loves.
45 All who came of his own age he conquered
At home and in the fine vale of Nisos' Hill.
    I am glad that all the city strives
For noble things.
Know this: through Menandros' fortune
A sweet recompense for your labours

Is yours. It is right that sportsmen
Should be made by a craftsman from Athens.
50 If you have come to sing of Themistios,
Shrink no longer. Give him your voice,

And spread out the sails on the topmost yard.
Proclaim that in boxing and the Trial of Strength
By his victory at Epidauros
He has won a twofold glory;
And to the porch of Aiakos
Bring the grassy garlands of flowers
And the long-haired Graces with you.

Nemean V was probably composed about 485 B.C. For the victor's family, see also *Isthmians V* and *VI*.

7 Aiakos was the son of Zeus and Aigina; his wife Endaïs (12) was the daughter of the Centaur Cheiron, who was the son of Kronos.

9 The Aiakidai are the founding fathers of Aigina and pray to Zeus as Father Hellanios.

12 ff. Phokos was the step-brother of Peleus and Telamon and treacherously killed by them. The killers had to leave Aigina, which is also called the Vineland.

13 The Sand-maiden, Psamatheia, daughter of Nereus and Doris, sleeps with Aiakos.

22 'those men also' – the Aiakidai. The Gods came to the wedding of Peleus and Thetis, and at it Apollo told in song how Peleus rejected the proposals of Hippolyta, daughter of Kretheus and wife of Akastos. She behaves like Potiphar's wife, but Peleus was saved by Zeus and given Thetis for wife.

36 The story of Thetis is told at greater length in *Isthmian VIII*. Poseidon, as competitor with Zeus for her hand, agrees to her marriage with Peleus.

41 Euthymenes is the uncle of Pytheas; Themistios is father of Enthymenes.

46 Nisos' Hill is at Megara.

48 ff. Menandros is the Athenian trainer of Pytheas.

53 The porch of Aiakos is his shrine in Aigina, where the wreaths of victory are dedicated.

ISTHMIAN VI

For Phylakidas of Aigina, winner in the boys'
trial of strength

I

As when men's revelry swells,
We mix a second bowl of the Muses' songs
In honour of Lampon's prize-winning family.
At Nemea first, O Zeus, for you
They gained the finest of garlands;
5 Now, in turn, for the Lord of the Isthmos
And the fifty Nereids
The youngest son, Phylakidas, is victor.
May a third time come
To make preparations for the Olympian Saviour on
    Aigina
And pour offerings of honey-voiced hymns.

10 For if any man delights in expense and effort
And sets in action high gifts shaped by the Gods,
And with him his destiny
Plants the glory which he desires,
Already he casts his anchor on the furthest edge of bliss,
And the Gods honour him.
In such a spirit Kleonikos' son
15 Prays to look in the face
And welcome death and old age. I address my words
To high-throned Klotho and her sister Fates,
To follow the noble commands
Of a man that I love.

For you, sons of Aiakos, on your gilded chariots,

20 I say that my clearest task
  Is to visit this island and drench it with words of praise.
  In fine doings countless roads
  Have been cut, a hundred feet wide, and stretch ahead
  Alike beyond the springs of Nile
  And through the People beyond the North.
  No city is so alien
  Or so harsh of tongue that it does not hear
25 Of the glory of the hero Peleus,
  Blessed son-in-law of the Gods,

II

  And of Aias and his father Telamon.
  Him did Alkmana's son
  Bring with men of Tiryns in ships
  To bronze-delighted war,
  An eager partner in battle,
  In a labour for heroes,
30 For the trespasses of Laomedon. He took
  Pergamos city, and with Telamon killed
  The breed of Meropes, and the herdsman like a moun-
      tain,
  Alkyoneus, whom he found at Phlegrai;
  Nor did Herakles spare with his hands
  His deep-voiced bow-string,

35 But when he called Aiakidas
  To take ship, he found young men feasting.
  Telamon bade Amphitryon's son, the mighty-speared,
  To stand on his lion-skin
  And begin the rite with pouring nectar.
  Peerless Telamon gave to him
40 A bowl, shivering with gold, full of wine.
  Herakles lifted his unconquerable hands to the sky

And spoke such a word: 'If ever, O father Zeus,
You have listened with glad heart to my prayers,

Now, I beg you, now,
With holy entreaties,
45   Bring to birth for this man a brave son
By Eriboia, to be my destined friend.
May he be unbroken in body,
As now prowls about me this skin of the beast
Which, first of all my labours,
I slew once in Nemea:
Let his heart be to match.' When thus he spoke,
50   The God sent a great eagle, lord of birds,
And sweet delight stung him within.

III

He lifted his voice and spoke like a prophet;
'Such a son as you ask, Telamon, you shall have,
And from the sight of this bird
Call him by name "Aias" with far-flung strength,
Terrible among men
In the toils of the Lord of the War Shout.'
55   So spoke he, and forthwith took his seat.
– But for me it is a long task
To rehearse all their acts of prowess.
    Muse, I have come for Phylakidas,
To dispense songs of revel for Pytheas
And for Euthymenes. In the Argive way
Their tale shall be told in the shortest words.

60   They have won victories in the Trial of Strength,
Three from the Isthmos, others from leafy Nemea,
The glorious sons and their mother's brother.
And what a portion of songs they have brought
To the daylight. Their land of the Psalychidai

They water with the loveliest dew of the Graces;
65 They have set up straight the house of Themistios,
And dwell in this city loved by the Gods.
Lampon gives care to his works
And pays high honour to the saying of Hesiod,
And commends it in speech to his sons.

He brings to his city honour among men;
70 He is loved for his kindnesses to strangers,
He keeps measure in his thoughts,
And measure in his doings;
Nor is his tongue outside his heart; you would say
That, a man among athletes,
He is among other stones
A Naxian whetstone to tame bronze.
I will pledge them
In the holy water of Dirka
Which the low-girdled daughters
75 Of golden-robed Memory
Set springing by the well-walled gates of Kadmos.

Isthmian VI was composed about 484 B.C. The victor, Phylakidas, son of Lampon, is brother of Pytheas, celebrated in *Nemean V*.

3 'Nemea' refers back to the victory celebrated in *Nemean V*.

5 The 'Lord of the Isthmos' is Poseidon.

7–9 Pindar suggests hopes of an Olympian victory in the future.

17 The Fates were Klotho, Lachesis, and Atropos.

22 The fame of the Aiakidai flies south to Egypt, north to the Hyperboreans.

26 ff. Telamon goes with Herakles to the first sack of Troy.

33 Alkyoneus is a giant, destroyed at Phlegrai in Chalkidike by Herakles and Telamon.

35–55 The myth tells how Herakles foretells the birth of Aias from Telamon's wife, Eriboia. His name Aias echoes the word for eagle, *aietos*.

58 Phylakidas wins at the Isthmos; Pytheas and Euthymenes, the boys'
uncle, at Nemea.

65 Themistios is the father of Euthymenes.

67 The line from Hesiod is *Works and Days* 412, 'trouble helps work'.

74 Pindar will honour Lampon and his sons with a song from Thebe

ISTHMIAN V

For Phylakidas of Aigina, winner in the
trial of strength

I

Mother of the Sun, Theia the many-named,
Because of you men prize gold in its great strength
Beyond all other possessions;
And in rivalry
5 Ships on the sea and horses in chariots
Are marvelled at, lady, because of your glory,
As they contend in fast-eddying races.

In the struggle of games he has won
The glory of his desire,
Whose hair is tied with thick garlands
10 For victory with his hands
Or swiftness of foot.
Men's valour is judged by their fates,
But two things alone
Look after the sweetest grace of life
Among the fine flowers of wealth, –

If a man fares well and hears his good name spoken.
  Seek not to become Zeus!
15 You have everything, if a share
Of these beautiful things comes to you.
Mortal ends befit mortal men.
– For you Phylakidas, at the Isthmos
A double success is planted and thrives,
And at Nemea for you and your brother Pytheas
In the Trial of Strength. My heart

Tastes song, and the Aiakidai help it.
20   I have come with the Graces
For the sons of Lampon

II

To this law-loving city.
If she has turned to a clean path
Of god-given actions,
25   Grudge not to mingle fitting praise
With song for her labours.
For among her heroes brave men of battle
Gained glory. They are renowned
On strings and the loud cries of flutes in every key

For uncounted time. Through Zeus
They were worshipped, and gave a theme
For craftsmen to work.
30   In the glowing sacrifices of the Aitolians
The strong sons of Oineus have honour, and at Thebes
Iolaos, driver of horses,
And Perseus at Argos,
And the spearmen Kastor and Polydeukes
By the streams of Eurotas,

But in the Vineland the high hearts
35   And tempers of Aiakos and his sons. Twice they sacked
The Trojans' city in battle,
First in the train of Herakles,
And then with Atreus' sons.
    Start now from the beginning, and tell
Who killed Kyknos, who Hektor,
40   And the fearless leader of the Ethiop host,
Memnon dressed in bronze? Who wounded
With his spear noble Telephos
By the banks of Kaïkos?

III

To them the lips of men assign
As fatherland Aigina, the surpassing island.
45 Long ago it was built as a tower
With walls for lofty prowess to climb.
My word-ready tongue has many arrows
To proclaim them aloud.
Now again in war the city of Aias could testify
That it has been set upright by its sailors,

Salamis, in the murderous storm of Zeus,
50 In the hail of blood of men past counting.
Nevertheless drench your boast in a rain of silence.
Zeus disposes this and that,
Zeus the master of everything.
In the sweet honey of song these honours also
Welcome the delight of a fine victory.
Let a man work and struggle

55 In the Games by studying
The breed of Kleonikos. The long toil
Of men is not lost in blindness.
Nor did counting the cost
Gnaw faith in their hopes.
I praise Pytheas also among those who master limbs,
60 For he has guided Phylakidas
On a straight course of boxing,
Skilled with his hands, with a mind to match them.
Take a wreath for him, and bring
A head-band of soft wool,
And with them send this new song on its wings.

Isthmian V may have been written in the autumn of 480 B.C. soon after
the battle of Salamis, in which the Aiginetans played a prominent part
in routing the Persian fleet. The victor is the same as in Isthmian VI.

1 Theia is traditionally the mother of the sun and the moon and therefore of light both physical and metaphorical, including the light of glory and vivid action.

17–19 There are four victories, two Isthmian and one Nemean, won by Phylakidas, and one Nemean (*Nemean VI*) won by Pytheas.

21 It is possible that Pindar came to Aigina for the performance of this song.

30 ff. Each great city has its special heroes, who are named with the Aiakidai of Aigina as the climax.

31 The sons of Oineus are Tydeus and Meleagros.

34 The Vineland is Aigina.

39 ff. Trojans and their allies killed in the Trojan War – Kyknos, son of Poseidon; Memnon, son of the Dawn; Telephos, king of Mysia: all killed by Achilles, who however is not named.

48 ff. The battle of Salamis, the island of Aias.

51 The command to keep silent is perhaps a caution against boasting too early before the Persians are finally driven out of Greece.

55 Kleonikos is father of Lampon and grandfather of Phylakidas.

ISTHMIAN VIII

For Kleandros of Aigina, winner in the boys'
trial of strength

I

For Kleandros and his stripling friends, young men,
In glorious release from his labours,
Let one of you go to the glittering doorway
Of his father Telesarchos
And awake the revel
As the prize of his Isthmian victory,
5 And for finding at Nemea mastery in the Games.
Wherefore I also, though with anguish at heart,
Am called to summon the golden Muse.
We have been freed from vast griefs;
So let us not give in and go without garlands;
Nor should you nurse sorrows. We have ended
Evils beyond contrivance
And shall give the people a sweet song
10 Even after our suffering;
For the stone of Tantalos
That hung over our head
Has been turned aside from us by some God,

II

An unendurable torment for Hellas. Yet
The passing of fear has delivered men
From overmastering cares. It is always best
15 To look at whatever lies before our feet;
For treacherous Time hangs over men
And twists awry the path of life. But even those things

Can be healed by men if freedom is with them;
And a man should give care to noble hope.
   One who is bred in seven-gated Thebes
Must pay the finest of songs to Aigina,
20 Because these are the twin eldest daughters
Among the children of father Asopos
And brought joy to Zeus the king.
One of them he made to dwell by the clear stream of
      Dirka,
And to govern a chariot-loving city.

III

But you he brought to the Vineland isle
And sent you to sleep; and there you bore
To the loud-thundering Father
25 Godlike Aiakos, finest of earth-men.
He accomplished what was right for the Gods.
His godlike sons and his sons' children
Delighted in war, and surpassed in courage
As they handled the brazen din of lamenting battle.
They were born modest and wise of heart.
This the assembly of the Blessed Ones remembered,
30 When Zeus and glorious Poseidon
Strove to marry Thetis,
Each wishing that she
Should be his beautiful bride.
Love held them in his grip.
But the Gods' undying wisdom
Would not let the marriage be,

IV

When they gave ear to the oracles. In their midst
35 Wise-counselling Themis said

That it was fated for the sea-goddess
To bear for son a prince
Stronger than his father,
Who shall wield in his hand a different weapon
More powerful than the thunderbolt
Or the monstrous trident,
If she wed Zeus or among the brothers of Zeus.
'Put an end to this. Let her have a mortal wedlock
40 And see dead in war her son
With hands like the hands of Ares
And feet like the lightning-flashes.
My counsel is: give her, a wedding-gift from the gods,
To Peleus, Aiakos' son
Whom, they say, the plain of Iolkos nurses,
Most god-fearing of men.

V

45 Let messages go forthwith
Straight to Cheiron's imperishable cave,
And let not Nereus' daughter
Twice set in our hands
The petals of strife. In evenings of full moon
She will unloose the lovely girdle of her virginity
To the hero.' So the Goddess
Spoke her message to Kronos' sons,
50 And with undying eyelids they consented:
Nor did the fruit of her words wither.
They say that the two Masters
Took thought for the common good and the wedding
        of Thetis.
The mouths of the wise revealed
To them that knew not the young valour of Achilles;
55 Who watered and stained the vines of the Mysian plain
With the black blood of Telephos,

VI

And bridged a return for Atreus' sons,
And set Helen free. With his spear
He hamstrung Troy's sinews; for they hampered him
As he ordered his task on the plain
Of slaying men in battle, – proud, violent Memnon,
60   And Hektor, and other champions. For them
Achilles, warder of the Aiakids,
Opened the house of Persephona
And made manifest Aigina and his beginnings.
Not even in death did songs forsake him,
But by his pyre and his tomb
The Maidens of Helikon stood and with many voices
Let flow a lament.
65   Even the Immortals thought fit to give
A brave man, though he was dead,
To Goddesses to chant in hymns.

VII

It is right now too, and the Muses' chariot
Hurries to its ringing memorial
Of Nikokles and his boxing. Honour him,
Who in the Isthmian valley
70   Won the Dorian parsley; for he too in his day
Defeated those from around as he tossed them with un-
erring hand.
He is not shamed by the son of his father's famous
brother.
Wherefore let one of his companions
Weave a delicate wreath of myrtle for Kleandros
In the Trial of Strength.
For strife and success at Alkathoos' Games,
75   And the young men of Epidauros welcomed him before;

He gives a good man occasion to praise him.
His youth is not unskilled in beautiful things,
And he has not buried it in a burrow.

Isthmian VIII seems to have been written in 478 B.C., soon after the withdrawal of the Persian army from Greece.

5–16 Pindar speaks of his own feelings. His own city of Thebes collaborated with the Persians, while his friends in Aigina took a leading part in opposing them. This personal distress which he compares with the stone hanging over the head of Tantalos (11) has just passed, and therefore there is a real call for rejoicing.

17 ff. The eponymous nymphs, Theba and Aigina, were both daughters of the river-god Asopos, and Pindar uses the relation to emphasize his own feelings of affection for Aigina, though he is a Theban. Theba wed Zeus and Aigina Poseidon.

26 ff. The Aiakidai, descendants of Aiakos, have the four cardinal virtues – courage, temperance, justice, and wisdom.

30–66 The myth of Thetis. Zeus and Poseidon both wish to marry her, but refrain because Themis prophesies that the child of such a union will be greater than his father. Let her marry the mortal Peleus, and she will bear Achilles, whose career is then sketched.

48 The full moon is the right time for a wedding.

55 The Mysian plain is that of Troy, and Telephos the king of Mysia.

62 ff. At the funeral of Achilles the Muses sang a dirge for him.

68 Nikokles is a kinsman of Kleandros. The reference to the memorial may mean that he has been killed at the battle of Salamis.

74 The Games of Alkathoos were at Megara.

ISTHMIANS III–IV

For Melissos of Thebes, winner in the chariot-race

III

I

If any man is fortunate, either
In glorious prizes or in the strength of wealth
And keeps down odious surfeit in his heart,
He is fit to be wedded to his townsmen's praises.
    Zeus, from you mighty qualities
5 Come to men. If they honour you,
Their happiness lasts longer,
But when it consorts with twisted minds
It flourishes not in like measure all the time.

In return for his glorious doings
We must sing of the noble man,
And in our revel we must exalt him with the gentle
    Graces.
10 It is the fate of Melissos in two contests
To turn his heart to sweet delight.
He has won wreaths in the vales of the Isthmus,
And in the hollow glen
Of the deep-chested lion
He proclaimed Thebes,

When he won in the racing of horses. He casts
No slur on the inborn worth of men.
15 You know the ancient renown
Of Kleonymos in chariots.
On their mother's side they are kin
To the Labdakidai

And walked through wealth
In their labour for four-horse teams.
But Time with its rolling days
Changes now this, now that.
Truly the sons of Gods are not to be wounded.

IV

I

By grace of the gods
I have an endless path
On every side; for you, Melissos, in the Isthmian Games
Have revealed to me abundant means
To pursue in song the prowess of your race.
In it the sons of Kleonymos
5 Have always flowered; a God helps them
As they come to the mortal end of life.
Many are the different winds
That rush down and drive all men.

From the beginning they were honoured
And told of at Thebes;
They were hosts to the dwellers around
And lacked loud-mouthed insolence.
10 All the testimonies of boundless glory
Of the dead and the living
That blow among men
They have clasped to perfection.
By uttermost works of manhood
From home they grip the Pillars of Herakles

They yearn not for further prowess beyond that.
They became breeders of horses
And delighted brazen Ares.
15 But on a single day

A happy hearth was robbed
Of four men by the rude snow-storm of war.
But now again, after the winter's murk,
The patterned earth has burst into blossom
20   With scarlet roses,

II

By the Gods' designs. The Mover of Earth,
Who dwells in Onchestos and the bridge of the sea
Before the walls of Korinth,
Gave this wonderful hymn to their race
And awakes from its bed their ancient renown
25   For glorious doings. It fell asleep,
But it stirs again
And is bright on the body
As the star of Dawn shines out among other stars.

It heralded their chariot-victory
In the fields of Athens;
And in the Games of Adrastos at Sikyon
It gave leaves of song, like mine, from men of those days,
30   Nor did they keep their curving car away
From the festivals where all men go,
But strove against all the Hellenes
And rejoiced in the cost of horses.
– Those who make no trial
Win silences that know them not.

Even for men who struggle Fortune
Stays undiscerned
Until they come to the lofty end;
35   She gives of this and of that.
The craft of worse men
Catches the better man and sends him sprawling. You
    know

Of the valour of Aias. He ripped it in blood
On his own sword late at night,
And brings reproach to all sons of the Hellenes
40 Who went to Troy.

III

But Homer has done him
Honour among men; for he set straight
All his prowess, and to his wand of celestial words
Told of it, to the delight of men to come.
For this goes forth undying in speech
45 If a man says a thing well.
Over the fruitful earth and across the sea
The sunbeam of fine doings has gone
Unquenchable for ever.

May we find the Muses in friendly mood, to kindle
That beacon-flame of songs for Melissos also,
A garland worthy of the Trial of Strength,
For the scion of Telesiadas. In struggle, at heart he is like
50 The daring of savage, loud-bellowing lions,
And in cunning a vixen,
Who hurls herself on her back
And withstands the eagle's swoop.
(A man must do everything
To wipe out his adversary.)

He had not the build of Orion,
But though he was poor to look at,
55 He was heavy to meet in encounter.
Once indeed to the house of Antaios from Kadmeian
    Thebes
Came a man short of stature, but in spirit
Unbreakable, to corn-bearing Libya
To wrestle with him,

That he might stop him from roofing
60 Poseidon's shrine with the skulls of strangers,

IV

The son of Alkmana. He came to Olympos,
After he had sought out
The deep-edged hollow of every land
And the grey sea, and tamed the Strait for sailing.
Now he dwells at the side of the Aegis-holder
65 In bliss most beautiful.
The Undying Ones have honoured him
As one whom they love, and Youth is his bride;
He dwells, a prince, in golden halls,
And Hera is his wife's mother.

To him above the Alektran gates
We citizens prepare a feast
And a newly built crown of altars.
We offer burnt sacrifice
For the death of eight bronze-clad sons,
70 Whom Kreon's daughter, Megara, bore to him.
In their honour when the daylight sinks
A flame rises and flares all night long,
Lashing the air with the smoke of sacrifice.

On the second day takes place
The decision of the yearly Games,
And strength gets to work. In them,
75 His head white with myrtle flowers,
This man has made known his two victories,
And a third before them among boys.
He has listened to the rich counsel and wisdom
Of the helmsman who guides the tiller.
With Orseas I shall sing of him in triumph
80 And scatter my grace and delight.

Isthmian IV was written, probably in 476 B.C., to celebrate the victory of Melissos in the chariot-race at the Isthmos. Soon afterwards he won the chariot-race at Thebes, and Pindar wrote *Isthmian III* and prefixed it to the other poem. This would be just before Pindar's departure for Sicily.

III. 9–10 Pindar refers to both victories won by Melissos.

12 The Nemean Games were held in the place where Herakles was thought to have killed the Nemean lion.

15 Kleonymos was an ancestor who won the chariot-race.

19 The sons of Gods may be wounded physically, but nothing affects their spirit.

IV. 12 The Pillars of Herakles, the present Straits of Gibraltar, marked the end of the known world and so, figuratively, of possible experience and effort.

16–18 Four members of the family have been killed in battle on a single day, presumably at Plataia, where the Thebans fought on the Persian side.

21 'The bridge of the sea' is on the Isthmus of Korinth, where the Isthmian Games were held. Onchestos was on the south edge of Lake Kopais in Boiotia; the modern name is Dimini.

28 Adrastos was thought to have founded the Games at Sikyon.

37 ff. Aias, by killing himself, brings dishonour to the Greeks at Troy, but Homer, by his generous treatment of him in the *Iliad*, has done something to restore his name. The story was that he killed himself because he felt dishonoured at not being given the armour of the dead Achilles.

53 ff. Melissos is short and stocky, and Herakles, much against the usual accounts, is said to be the same.

56 ff. Antaios was a Giant, who derived his strength from contact with the earth. Herakles lifted him up and so defeated him. He was the son of Poseidon and decorated his father's temple with the heads of strangers.

62 After death Herakles was translated to Olympos.

67 ff. The song must have been sung at a festival by the Alektran Gates of Thebes, which were connected with the slaughter of his children by Herakles in a fit of madness.

79 Orseas is the trainer of Melissos.

OLYMPIAN XI

For Hagesidamos of Western Lokroi, winner in the boys' boxing

There is a time when men's strongest need
Is for the winds, and a time for the sky's water,
The clouds' showery children.
If anyone toils and succeeds,
Sweet voices of song
5   Are paid on account for words to come
And a faithful pledge to surpassing actions.

Beyond grudging, this praise
Is laid up for Olympian victors. Such themes
My tongue loves to tend,
10 But it is God who makes a man
To flower as his wise mind wishes.
Know now, son of Archestratos,
Hagesidamos, because of your boxing

I shall sing a sweet song
To be a jewel in your crown of golden olive,
15 And honour the Western Lokrians' race.
Join there in the revel! I shall give my word,
Muses, that he will not come
To a host that puts strangers to flight
Or knows not beautiful things;
They stand on wisdom's height and are soldiers.
– Its inborn ways neither the tawny fox
20 Shall change, nor loud-bellowing lions.

Olympian XI was composed in 476 B.C. and probably sung at Olympia soon after the victory.

5 This is Pindar's promise that he will compose a full epinician later for Hagesidamos. This he does, a little later, in *Olympian X*.

17 Read μιν, not μέν.

OLYMPIAN I

For Hieron of Syracuse, winner in the horse-race

1

Water is the best thing of all, and gold
Shines like flaming fire at night,
More than all a great man's wealth.
But if, my heart, you would speak
Of prizes won in the Games,
5 Look no more for another bright star
By day in the empty sky
More warming than the sun,
Nor shall we name any gathering
Greater than the Olympian.
The glorious song of it is clothed by the wits of the
    wise:
10 They sing aloud of Kronos' son,
When they come to the rich and happy hearth of
    Hieron,

Who sways the sceptre of law
In Sicily's rich sheep-pasture.
He gathers the buds of all perfections,
15 And his splendour shines in the festal music,
Like our own merry songs
When we gather often around that table of friends.
    But take down from its peg the Dorian lute,
If surely the beauty of Pisa, the beauty of Pherenikos,
Loaded our hearts with the sweetest thoughts,
20 When by Alpheios he raced past,
Giving his strength in the course, not waiting for the
    spur,

And brought to triumph his master,

The King of Syracuse, the soldier-horseman.
His fame is bright in the great assembly of men
Which Lydian Pelops founded:
25 – He, with whom the mighty Earth-Shaker Poseidon
       fell in love,
When Klotho lifted him out of the cleansing cauldron,
With his shoulder of ivory, white and fine.
There are many wonders, and it may be
Embroidered tales overpass the true account
And trick men's talk
With their enrichment of lies.

II

30 Beauty, who creates
All sweet delights for men,
Brings honour at will and makes the false seem true
Time and again; but the wisest witness of all
Are the days to come.
35 Let a man speak good of the Gods,
And his blame shall be less.
   Son of Tantalos, in my tale of you
I shall counter the poets before me.
When your father called his companions
To his most innocent banquet, and to Sipylos his home,
Making the Gods his guests, who had made him theirs,
40 Then the bright Trident's God

Lost his heart for love of you, and seized you,
And carried you on his golden mares
To the high house of wide-worshipped Zeus:
Where later in time Ganymedes came also
45 For the same service to Zeus.
When you were no more seen and men searched long

But brought you not home to your mother,
Then some envious neighbour told the tale in secret,
That the water bubbled over the fire
And they sliced you into it
Limb by limb with a knife.
50 Then at the second course of the feast
They portioned the meat of your body and ate.

I cannot say, not I,
That any Blessed God has a gluttonous belly –
I stand aside.
Those who speak evil have troubles thick upon them:
And if the watchers on Olympos
Ever showed honour to a mortal man,
55 Tantalos was he. And yet
His stomach could not hold such mighty fortune:
He came to huge mischief,
– A mighty rock, which the Father hung over him,
And longing always to cast it from his head,
He is exiled from delight.

III

Without strength he lives, in eternal trouble,
60 And has with three torments a fourth, because he stole
And gave to his companions who drank with him
The Gods' nectar and ambrosia
With which they made him immortal.
The man who thinks that he will do anything
And God not see is wrong.
65 Therefore the Immortals thrust back his son
Among men to whom death comes soon;
And when he came to the sweet flower of his growth
And down covered his darkening chin,
He lifted his thoughts to a bridal awaiting him,

70 To have far-famed Hippodameia
From her Pisatan father.
He went down beside the grey sea
In the darkness alone,
And cried to the loud-bellowing Lord of the Trident.
And the God was with him
Close beside his feet: and Pelops said:
75 'If the dear love you had of me, Poseidon,
Can turn, I pray, to good,
Keep fast now the brazen spear of Oinomaos,
And on the swiftest chariots carry me
To Elis and bring me to victory;
For he has slain thirteen men that wooed her,
80 And puts back the bridal day

Of his daughter. The danger is great
And calls not the coward: but of us who must die,
Why should a man sit in darkness
And cherish to no end
An old age without a name,
Letting go all lovely things?
For me this ordeal waits: and you,
85 Give me the issue I desire.'
So he spoke, and the prayer he made was not un-
answered.
The God glorified him, and gave him a chariot of gold
And winged horses that never tired.

IV

So he brought down the strength of Oinomaos,
And the maiden to share his bed.
She bore him princes,
Six sons very eager in nobleness.
And now by the Ford of Alpheos

90 He is drenched in the glorious blood-offerings,
With a busy tomb beside that altar
Where strangers throng past number.
The fame of the Olympiads in the Games of Pelops
Overlooks the wide earth.
95 There a man's strong prime endures its toils,
And the victor all his remaining days
Breathes a delicious and serene air

When he remembers the Games.
And yet these good things
100 That come with each day as it comes
Are still the best of all for all men.
I must crown the victor with the Horsemen's Tune
In my Aeolian melody.
I know well there is no friend of strangers
Among men alive
Greater than he, whether in knowledge
Of all good things or in power,
105 For me to enrich in the splendid folds of song.
God is your guardian, Hieron:
He charges himself with this, and watches over all your
cares,
And if he desert you not soon,
I hope to find a sweeter path even

110 And to join with a swift chariot in giving you glory,
When I come along the path that awakens speech,
To Kronos' Hill standing in the sun.
The Muse is nursing for me a javelin
Marvellously valiant and strong.
One man is great in this way, another in that,
But at the peak of all
Are Kings. Look no farther than this.
115 I pray you may walk exalted

All these days of your life,
And may I so long keep company with victors,
A beacon-light of song
Among the Hellenes everywhere.

Olympian I was written in 476 B.C. and performed at Syracuse at the court of Hieron in the presence of Pindar.

1 As water, gold, and the sun are each in their spheres supreme, so in athletics is a victory in the Olympian Games.

4 Pindar speaks to himself as 'my heart'.

17 Pindar again addresses himself.

18 The horse Pherenikos, which has won the horse-race, had also won in the Pythian Games in 482 and 478 B.C.

18 Pisa is near Olympia and next to the actual racing-ground.

24 ff. Pindar prepares the way for his rejection of the myth that Tantalos served up his son Pelops as a dish for the gods, and that Damater ate the shoulder, for which afterwards, when the boy was brought back to life, an ivory shoulder was substituted. This was allegedly to be seen at Olympia. Pindar's words are as yet ambiguous and fit both the old version and his own revision of it.

36 ff. The new version is that Poseidon fell in love with Pelops and spirited him off to Olympos.

46 ff. The current legend is explained as the invention of gossip.

52 Pindar refuses to admit that Damater could, out of greed, have eaten Pelops' shoulder.

55 ff. The doom of Tantalos. He abuses the Gods' kindness to him, and tries to make his companions immortal by giving them nectar and ambrosia.

60 His three punishments are hunger, thirst, and the stone over his head, and the fourth is that they last for ever.

65–93 In contrast with Tantalos, who is an example of how wrong a king can go, is his son Pelops, who is favoured by the Gods. He is sent back to earth after his father's fall, but there Poseidon continues to help him, by giving him horses which defeat Oinomaos and win him Hippodameia for bride. The west pediment of the temple of Zeus at Olympia shows the situation just before the chariot-race, which Pelops won by bribing the charioteer of Oinomaos to loosen the lynch-pins in his master's chariot.

90 Pelops was worshipped at Olympia with blood-offerings.

101 The Horsemen's Tune was a traditional melody associated with Kastor and Polydeukes.

109–11 Pindar expresses a hope that in due course Hieron will win the chariot-race at Olympia and ask Pindar to celebrate it in song. Hieron in fact won the race in 468 B.C., but did not ask Pindar to celebrate it. See *Pythian II*.

NEMEAN I

For Chromios of Aitna, winner in the horse-race

I

Holy place where Alpheos breathes again,
Green branch of glorious Syracuse,
Ortygia, in whom Artemis sleeps,
Sister of Delos,
From you the hymn's sweet words set out
5 To lift the strong praise of storm-footed horses
For the sake of Zeus of Aitna:
And Chromios' car and Nemea press me
To yoke a triumphant tune
To his victorious doings.

My beginnings are laid in the Gods
With that man's predestined prowess.
10 In success is the top
Of world-wide glory, and the Muse
Loves to remember great Games.
Scatter then a brightness on the island
Which Zeus, master of Olympos,
Gave to Persephona,
And to her with his locks consented
To exalt on high, surpassing the fruitful earth,

15 Sicily, teeming with wealthy peaks
Of cities.
The Son of Kronos gave her
A people of horsemen
To make love to bronze-armoured war –
And often indeed to have fastened on them

The Olympian olive's golden leaves.
I have struck a chance to say much,
And I touch nothing with falsehood.

II

I have taken my stand at the courtyard-gate
20 Of a man who welcomes strangers,
And sweet is my song.
Here a fitting feast is set; not often
Is the house without guests from over sea.
– He has found good men
To quench with water the smoke of cavil.
25   Many are the arts of men,
But we must walk on straight ways
And fight by our own blood.

Action sets strength to work,
And counsel the mind
In those who by their breed foresee what is coming.
   Son of Hagesidamos, in your nature lies
30 The use of the one and the other.
I do not lust to hide great wealth
And keep it in a store-room,
But of my stock to live well
And win a good name to my friends' delight.
For to all comes a share in the hopes

Of those who toil hard. Gladly I cling
To Herakles
On the tall peaks of prowess
And awake an ancient tale,
35 How when the son of Zeus
Came straight from his mother's womb
To the glittering daylight
And with his twin-brother escaped the pangs of birth,

III

From her golden throne Hera failed not to see him
When he was swaddled in his saffron baby-clothes.
40 The Queen of the Gods was angry at heart
And at once sent snakes,
Which passed through the open doors
Into the chamber's wide space,
Eager to writhe their quick jaws
Around the children. But *he*
Lifted his head on high and made first trial of battle.

In two unescapable hands
45 He seized the two serpents by their necks:
He strangled them, and his grip
Squeezed the life out of their unspeakable frames.
Then unbearable terror smote the women,
All who were there to help Alkmana in childbed.
Unclothed as she was,
She jumped to her feet from her blankets
And would ward off the arrogant brutes.

50 Quickly the Kadmeians' princes,
One and all,
Raced up with bronze weapons;
Amphitryon came and shook
A naked sword from its sheath.
Piercing pangs struck him; for every man
Feels the burden of what is his own,
But for another's trouble
The heart soon ceases to fret.

IV

55 He stood dumbfounded in wonder
Hard to endure but delightful.

He saw the surpassing spirit and strength of his son.
The Undying Ones had turned
The messengers' tale to falsehood.
60 He called for his neighbour,
Chief interpreter of most high Zeus,
Teiresias, prophet of truth,
Who told him and all the company
With what fortunes the boy shall consort,

How many he shall slay on dry land,
How many wicked, wild beasts in the sea,
'And one who sidles in surfeit
65 And walks the most hateful of men,'
He said, 'he shall give to his doom.
For when on Phlegra's plain
The Gods meet the Giants in battle
Bright hair shall be fouled in the dust
Under the gale of his arrows,'

He told, 'but he for the whole of time
Unending
70 Shall win calm as the choice reward of his mighty labours
In the Halls of the Blest.
He shall have tender Youth for bride,
And feast at his wedding with Zeus Kronidas
And praise the ways of the Holy.'

Nemean I was written in 476 B.C. and performed at Syracuse soon after
Pindar's arrival (19 ff.). Chromios was a veteran soldier who had served
Hieron in his wars.

1 The river Alpheos, which flows past Olympia, was believed to pass
under the sea and reappear as the fountain Arethoisa at Syracuse.

2 Ortygia is the island part of Syracuse, which was early joined to the
mainland.

4 Ortygia is sister of Delos because both have a cult of Artemis.

6 Hieron refounded Katana as Aitna and established a cult of Zeus of Aitna.

13 Sicily was the wedding-gift of Zeus to Persephona.

24 This means that Chromios has friends to protect him from slander.

33 Herakles is introduced as the subject for the myth. He was much honoured in Sicily. Pindar tells his story in the form of a prophecy made by Teiresias just after his birth.

39 Hera is jealous of Alkmana, Herakles' mother, and sends snakes to kill the child.

63–5 It is not clear who this is. Alkyoneus is a possibility.

67–8 Herakles, fighting for the Gods against the Giants, is depicted on the frieze of the Siphnian Treasury at Delphoi.

OLYMPIAN III

For Theron of Akragas, winner in the chariot-race

I

To please Tyndareos' sons, the friends of strangers,
And lovely-haired Helen is my prayer,
And to honour famous Akragas,
While I set up for Theron
An Olympian victory-song, the choicest honour
For his horses whose hooves never weary.
For this the Muse has taken her stand at my side,
And I have found a new and glittering way
5   To fit to a Dorian sandal the voice

Of the choir's praises. For garlands
Bound on the hair exact from me
This holy debt,
To mingle in honour fit for Ainesidamos' sons
The harp's many notes,
The flute's cry, and the patterned words,
And Pisa makes me cry his name aloud.
10   Thence by God's will songs come to men

In honour of him on whose hair
The strict Aetolian arbiter,
Fulfilling the ancient orders of Herakles,
Sets the olive's pale-skinned ornament,
Which once Amphitryon's son
Brought from Ister's shadowy springs
To be the finest remembrance
15   Of the Games at Olympia.

II

His words beguiled Apollo's servants,
The People living beyond the North,
When with candid heart
He begged for the all-welcoming grove of Zeus
A shady tree for men to share
And to be the crown for prowess.
Already the Father's altars were sanctified,
And at the middle of the month in the evening
The gold-charioted moon
20 Kindled her round eye for him.

He had set up the holy trial
In the great Games
And the Feast of the Fourth Year also,
On Alpheos' holy rocks.
But in the valleys of Kronos' Hill
The acre of Pelops was not green with beautiful trees:
Naked of them, the garden seemed to him
At the mercy of the sun's sharp rays.
25 Then did his spirit stir him
To journey to the land

Of Ister. There he came
From Arkadia's ridges and twisting valleys;
And Lato's daughter, driver of horses,
Welcomed him, when on the command of Eurystheus
A doom laid by his father
Drove him in search of the doe with golden horns,
Which once Taÿgeta offered in her own stead
30 Holy to the Orthian Maid.

III

In pursuit of it he saw that land
Behind the blasts of the cold north wind;

77

There he stood and marvelled at the trees.
Sweet desire for them seized him,
To plant them on the edge of the horses' track
Where the chariots drive twelve times round.
   And graciously now he comes
To this our feast
With low-girdled Leda's children,
35 Twins and peers of the Gods.

To them, when he went to Olympos,
He entrusted the rule
Of the splendid struggle
In men's worth and fast chariot-driving.
   My heart stirs me to say
That the glory come to Theron and to the Emmenidai
Is the gift of the horsemen, Tyndareos' sons,
Because most of all mankind they welcome them
40 At their table with entertainment,

And guard with humble hearts
The mysteries of the Blessed Ones.
   Even as water is best
And gold the most honoured of treasures,
So now Theron has come to the verge by his prowess
And reaches from home
To the Pillars of Herakles.
What is beyond may not be trodden
By wise or unwise.
45 I shall not chase it, – a fool's game!

Olympian III was written in 476 B.C. and performed at Akragas, of which the victor, Theron, was tyrant, at a semi-religious feast at which the Dioskouroi and their sister, Helen, were believed to be present.

6 Garlands are worn to show the special nature of the occasion.

9 Theron was the son of Ainesidamos.

11–34 The myth concerns the olive-trees at Olympia. A crown of olive was the prize for victory, and Pindar tells how Herakles brought the trees from the Hyperboreans.

14 The river Ister has been identified with the Danube, but also with other rivers further north.

16 That Herakles got the trees by words seems unlikely, and we may suspect that Pindar has tempered a more vigorous story.

26 ff. Herakles reaches the Hyperboreans in his pursuit of the doe with golden horns, who was the Pleiad Taÿgeta after she was transformed by Artemis to escape the attentions of Zeus.

42 This looks like an echo from the opening lines of *Olympian I* and may well be deliberate.

OLYMPIAN II

For Theron of Akragas, winner in the chariot-race

I

Lords of the harp, my songs,
Of what God, of what Hero,
Of what Man shall our music be?
Pisa belongs to Zeus, the Olympian feast
Herakles founded, the loot of war,
5   But of Theron let your voices ring,
For his victorious four-in-hand.
He is courteous and kind to guests,
The bulwark of Akragas;
In him his famous fathers
Flower, and the city stands.

They suffered much in their hearts to win
A holy home on the river,
10 And were the eye of Sicily;
The destined days
Came adding wealth and joy
To their trueborn nobleness.
   Son of Kronos and Rhea,
Lord of a seat on Olympos and the Hill of the Games
And the Ford of Alpheos,
Rejoice in my songs, and in friendliness
Guide still their ancestral fields

15 For the generations to come.
Of what has been done
In right or against right
Not even Time, father of everything,

Can undo the accomplishment;
In good luck and fortune
Forgetfulness will come;
For in noble delights sorrow perishes
20 Angry but overwhelmed,

II

When God's fate tips the scale of happiness high.
   This word fits the high-throned daughters of Kad-
      mos.
Greatly they suffered, but heavy grief
Falls under conquering blessings.
25 Among the Olympians she lives who died
In the thunderbolt's crash,
Long-haired Semela: Pallas
Loves her for ever, and father Zeus, and exceedingly
Her ivy-crowned boy loves her.

They say that in the sea also
Among the sea-maidens, the daughters of Nereus,
30 Unperishing life has been ordained for Ino
For the whole of time.
Truly no mark is set for the death of men,
Nor when we shall close the quiet day, the Sun's child,
With unfaltering joy.
Many are the streams that come to men,
Now with the heart's delight, and now with sorrow.

35 So Fate, who holds for them the friendly fortune
That their fathers had,
With heaven-born joy brings grief,
Itself to turn about with time;
Ever-since his doomed son encountered Laios
And killed him, fulfilling the oracle
40 Spoken in Pytho long before.

III

The sharp-eyed Fury saw
And destroyed the warrior-race
In slaughter one of another.
Polyneikes fell, but he left Thersandros,
Honoured in young men's games and in battles of war,
45   A shoot from Adrastos' stock, who succoured his house.
    With his root from that seed
  It is right that Ainesidamos' son
  Should find songs of praise and the harp.

For at Olympia he
Won the prize himself; at Pytho and the Isthmos
50   The impartial Graces made his brother
Share his portion in the flowers
For the chariot racing twelve times round.
(To win the game by trying
Saves a man from the name of fool.)
Truly wealth patterned with prowess
Brings the moment for this or for that,
If it rouses deep ambition to range afar,

55   A transcendent star, the truest light for a man.
    If any man has it, and knows what shall come, –
  That of those who die here
  The lawless souls at once pay penalty,
  And sins done in this kingdom of Zeus
  Are judged by one below earth
60   With harsh inexorable doom.

IV

But in nights like ours for ever,
With a like sun in their days,
The good win a life without labour,

Nor brace their hands to trouble earth
65   Or the sea's water for an empty livelihood.
Beside the most honoured of Gods
Those who delighted to keep their word
Pass unweeping days; the others
Support a burden not to be looked upon.

All who have endured three times
In a sojourn in either world,
70   To keep their souls utterly clean of wrong,
Go by God's road to the Tower of Kronos,
Where the Airs, daughters of Ocean,
Blow round the Island of the Blest,
And the flowers are of gold,
Some on land flaming from bright trees,
Others the water feeds;
They bind their hands with them and make garlands,

75   In the straight rule of Rhadamanthys,
Whom the great Father keeps at his side in counsel,
The husband of Rhea on her all-highest throne.
Peleus and Kadmos are in that number;
Achilles too was brought by his mother,
80   When she moved the heart of Zeus with prayers.

V

He overthrew Hektor, Troy's
Unconquerable, unshaken pillar,
And Kyknos he gave to death,
And the Dawn's Ethiopian son.
   In the quiver under my elbow
85   Are many swift arrows that speak to the wise,
But for the crowd they need interpreters.
He knows, whose blood tells him much;

Mere learners babble, the pair of them,
And like crows chatter vainly against

God's holy bird.
  Now keep the bow on the mark.
Come, my heart, at whom do we aim
90 And shoot from a gentle heart our shafts of glory?
At Akragas I draw, and I shall speak
My words on oath with an honest mind: –
In a hundred years this city has borne
No man more lavish in heart to his friends,
More open of hand,

95 Than Theron. Yet against my praise
Surfeit advances, not companioned
By right, but in gluttonous mouths,
And wishes to make its prattle
Cover up the fine doings of men.
– Since sand escapes all counting,
Of *his* gifts to others
100 Who could recount the tale?

Olympian II was written at about the same time as *Olympian III*, also for Theron, but possibly for a more intimate occasion.

8–10 Theron's ancestors came from Rhodes.

22 The daughters of Kadmos, Semela and Ino, are examples of ill fortune being turned to good.

25–7 Semela, mother of Dionysos, the 'ivy-crowned boy' (27), was killed by lightning.

38 The 'doomed son of Laios' is Oidipous, whose sons, Eteokles and Polyneikes (42), kill one another, but the family survives in Thersandros, who takes part in the War of the Successors after the failure of the Seven against Thebes, who included Adrastos.

49 The brother of Theron is Xenokrates, known from *Pythian VI* and *Isthmian II*.

56–83 Instead of a myth Pindar tells of life after death in language which suggests cults in Sicily and Theron's own beliefs.

59 'One below earth' is the judge of the dead, not named because he is not to be spoken of.

61–6 The abode of the good, with days and nights like ours.

68–80 The Isle of the Blest, with no clear geographical setting.

75 Rhadamanthys, the incarnation of justice, holds rule.

76 The 'great father' is Kronos, who has Rhea at his side.

83 Pindar breaks off his revelations and turns to personalities. Theron must be 'the wise', who will understand what Pindar says. The ancient commentators identify the 'crows' with the poets Simonides and Bacchylides, who were in Sicily at this time.

PYTHIAN IX

*For Telesikrates of Kyrene, winner in the
race in armour*

I

I wish to proclaim aloud
The bronze-shielded Pythian victor;
And the deep-zoned Graces shall help me cry his name
Telesikrates! fortunate man, crowning the brows
5 Of Kyrene, the horse-taming maiden: her, whom once
Lato's long-haired son
Snatched from the wind-swept glades of Pelion.
Carrying her off, wild girl,
In a golden chariot, he made her queen
Of a country of many flocks and all kinds of fruits,
To inhabit the third fixed continent of earth
And blossom in a lovely land.

Silver-footed Aphrodita
10 Received her guest from Delos,
Laying a light hand
On his chariot built in heaven:
And throwing on their sweet bed
The shamefastness of love
She made one marriage
For the God alike and the daughter of mighty Hypseus.
(He was king in those days of the presumptuous Lapiths,
A hero, grandson of Ocean.
15 In the storied valleys of Pindos
The Naiad Kreoisa, in joy at her love of Peneios,

The daughter of Earth,

86

Bore him; and he
Bred up the strong-armed child Kyrene.)
She loved not to walk to and fro before the loom
Nor the delight of feasting with her companions
Who kept the house:
20 But with javelins of brass and a sword
She fought and slew wild beasts,
And gave great peace and quiet
To her father's herds: niggard was she,
Letting her sweet bedfellow,
Sleep, brush her eyes but briefly, towards the dawn.

II

The God of the Broad Quiver found her:
Whilst she was wrestling once
Alone with a strong lion, without her spears,
Far-shooting Apollo came on her.
Thereat with a shout
He called Cheiron out of his dwelling,
30 'Leave your dread cave, son of Philyra, and be amazed
At the courage and great strength of a woman.
Look what a fight she makes, her head unflinching,
Her maiden spirit high
Above the struggle:
Fear makes no storm in her heart.
What mortal begot her? From what stock was she torn

To dwell in the folds of the shadowy hills, and sound
35 Her unplumbed depths of valour?
Were it no sin to lay my mighty hand on her
And take the delicious pasture of her love?'
With softened eyes, the huge Centaur
Dewily laughed: swift and wise was his answer:
'They are secret keys

With which Persuasion knows how to unlock
The sanctuaries of love,
40 Phoibos: Gods and men are alike
Shy of it being spoken of, when first they come
To some sweet maidenhead.

So you, whom untruth may not touch,
Were led in the honey-sweetness of your mood
To speak with guile.
You ask of what race the girl is –
You, Sir, who know
45 The appointed end of all, and all paths:
How many leaves in April the earth puts forth,
How many grains of sand
In the sea and in the rivers
Are troubled by the waves and the swirling winds,
And what shall be, and whence it shall come,
You see with clear eyes.
50 If I must match my own wisdom with that,

III

I will speak:
You came to this glade to wed her,
And you will carry her over the sea
To the chosen garden of Zeus.
You will make her there a queen of cities,
55 Gathering an island people
To a hill amidst a plain, but now
Among wide meadows the Lady Libya
Shall welcome her, your glorious bride,
In gold palaces gladly.
She shall give her at once, that she may dwell beside her,
A portion of land
To yield her fruit of all that grows,

88

And wild beasts shall be found there.

There she shall bear her child:
And Hermes the great God shall carry him
60   Away from his loving mother
To the high-throned Hours, and to Earth; and they,
Gazing at the fair infant on their knees,
Shall on his lips drop nectar and ambrosia
And make him undying.
His name shall be Zeus and holy Apollo,
The delight of them that love him: close at hand
65   To follow the flock, Hunter and Shepherd:
And others shall call him Aristaios.'
He spoke, and aroused Apollo
To reach the sweet fulfilment of his marriage.

When Gods are once in haste,
Their work is swift, their ways short:
That day, that day determined it.
In Libya's rich golden room
They lay together; and there
70   She is keeper of a city
Surpassing lovely, and famous in the Games.
And now in fair Pytho Karneiadas' son
Has grafted on her a flowering fortune.
There he won and proclaimed Kyrene:
And she will be kind and welcome him
To his land of fair women
75   From Delphoi, with his lovely spoil of glory.

IV

Great deeds give choice of many tales.
Choose a slight tale, enrich it at large, and then
Let wise men listen! Yet to all alike
The Moment gives the crown;

Whose favour was shown of old
In seven-gated Thebes
80 To Iolaos, that with the edge of his sword
Cut off Eurystheus' head; and then
Was hid deep in earth, in the grave
Of the chariot-driver Amphitryon
His father's father: who lay, the Spartoi's guest,
Where he came once to live
In the Kadmeians' cavalcaded streets.

With him, and with Zeus, proud Alkmana lay,
85 And at one travail
Bore twin sons, strong prevailers in war.
　Dumb is that man who does not turn aside
For Herakles his tongue,
Or ever forgets the waters of Dirka
Which nursed him and Iphikles.
To them I will lead the procession:
I asked for a blessing, and they gave it me entire:
90 'Let not the pure light
Of the singing Graces forsake me.'
In Aigina, I say,
And on the hill of Nisos,
Having three times brought glory to this city

I have escaped dumb helplessness indeed.
Therefore let friends in this city, and enemies too,
Not hide
This labour for the good of all well spent.
Let them maintain the word
Of the Old Man of the Sea:
95 'Praise your enemy also
Who heartily, and in righteousness, does well.'
　Often, too, you have won
At the returning mysteries of Pallas:

While maidens watched, and in silence each one wished
You, Telesikrates,
100 Were her dearest husband, or her son;

V

And at the Olympia, and the Games
Of deep-bosomed Earth,
Yes all the Games of your country.
Here is one, whose thirst I am quenching with song,
Demands his due, bids me again awake
105 The ancient fame of his fathers.
– For a Libyan woman's sake
They came to the city of Irasa, – her suitors,
Antaios' lovely-haired, far-famous child.
She was sought by many a paladin, her kinsmen
And many strangers besides:
For marvellous beauty

Was hers: and they longed to gather the blossoming
fruit
110 Of her maidenhood, its crown of gold.
But her father was planning for his daughter
A finer wedding: he heard
How Danaos once in Argos could achieve
For his eight and forty daughters,
Before midday, a wedding swift indeed.
For he stood them all, then and there,
At the end of the lists: and bade these heroes,
115 Who had come to wed them,
Decide by foot-race which each man should have.

So too the Libyan offered, when he would choose
A bridegroom for his child,
He stood her on the line, arraying her

To be their far goal,
And made proclamation in their midst:
He who first leaped forward
120 And touched the folds of her garments
Should lead her away for his own.
There did Alexidamos
Come clear of the swift race
And took the maiden princess, hand in his hand:
He led her through the host of the Nomad horsemen.
Many were the leaves and the garlands
They threw on him,
125 And many the wings of victory
He had won before.

Pythian IX was written in 474 B.C. and performed at Thebes, where the victor, Telesikrates, seems to have stopped on his way back to Kyrene.

5–69 The myth of the eponymous nymph Kyrene.

10 The 'guest from Delos' is Apollo.

14–16 The ancestry of Kyrene.

30–37 Apollo's questions about Kyrene are, as Cheiron shows, not needed, but made in a playful mood.

55 This refers to the later colonization of Kyrene by Greeks from Thera.

59 ff. Kyrene's child, Aristaios, is a local god, who is identified with Zeus and Apollo and also has his own agricultural titles.

73 Telesikrates will go to Kyrene in due course, but at present he is in Thebes.

79 Iolaos and Amphitryon are buried in Thebes, near the Spartoi, who were sprung from the Dragon's teeth sown by Jason.

89–96 Pindar defends himself against some not very specific charge, presumably that he has been too generous to Athens, whom he praised in a famous Dithyramb, and who was a traditional enemy of Thebes. For this he was said to have been heavily fined. The whole passage has little to do with Telesikrates and illustrates how Pindar uses a public occasion to speak about his own affairs.

91 For εὐκλέϊξας read εὐκλεΐξαι.

105–25 A second myth, which tells how Alexidamos wins a wife by his swift running. The story seems to be of local Kyrenian origin, and Alexidamos to have been an ancestor of Telesikrates.

111–14 Danaos was compelled to marry his daughters to Egyptians who pursued them with violence. See *Nemean X 6.*

Since both myths speak of marriage, it seems possible that Telesikrates was about to be married.

PYTHIAN III

For Hieron of Syracuse

I

I could wish
That Cheiron, Philyra's son,
(If with my lips I should utter all men's prayer)
Were alive, who is departed,
The lord of wide lands, the seed of Kronos Ouranidas,
– That he ruled in the glades of Pelion, the wild Centaur,
5 With a heart friendly to man:
As he was when he nursed
The gentle worker of sound-limbed painlessness,
Asklapios the hero,
Healer of every sickness.

Him the daughter of Phlegyas the great horseman
Had not brought to birth
With Eleithyia to tend her,
When she was struck by the golden arrows
10 Of Artemis: in her chamber she went down
To the house of Death
By the device of Apollo.
It is not idle, the anger of Zeus' children –
But she,
Making light of it in the folly of her soul,
Must needs wed with another, cheating her sire,
She who had lain already with long-haired Phoibos

15 And bore the God's pure seed.
She would not wait the coming of the marriage-meal
Nor for the shout of many voices,

The Bride's song, that her friends, the girls of her age,
As the night falls, will sing to their playmate.
20 – Not she: she was after what was not there,
As many have been; vain heads all the sort of them,
Who disdain home things and cast their glance afar,
Chasing the empty air, with hopes
Which they cannot attain.

II

Like that was the great blindness of the soul
25 Of lovely-robed Koronis.
For a stranger came
From Arkadia, and she lay in his bed: but the Watcher
saw her.
By the sheep-altar in Pytho, the temple's King
Loxias, standing, was aware of her.
A most instant helper made him sure,
His All-knowing Mind:
Which holds no traffic with lies: no God, no man de-
ceives it
30 Either in word or in plan.

Yea, then he perceived
How with Ischys son of Elatos,
A stranger, she lay, sinning deceitfully,
He sent his sister storming in terrible strength
To Lakereia: for there
Where the hills slope down to Boibias Lake
The girl was dwelling. Changed now was the doom
35 That turned her to evil and overcame her.
Many were they of her neighbours
Who felt that stroke and died with her:
(Much is the timber on the hillside
That fire destroys, leaping from a single seed).

But when her kinsmen set the girl
On the piled logs
40 And the hungry light of the Fire God ran around,
Then Apollo spoke:
'No more can my spirit endure
To destroy my child by this most pitiful death
After his mother's anguish.'
– He spoke, and with one stride came
And out of the dead body snatched the child:
The flaming pyre blazed either side of him.
He bore him away and gave him
45 To the Magnesian Centaur: there he should learn
To heal the divers pains of the sicknesses of men.

III

All who came
Bound fast to sores which their own selves grew,
Or with limbs wounded, by grey bronze
50 Or a far-flung stone, or wasting in body with summer
    fire, or with winter
He, loosing all from their several sorrows,
Delivered them. Some he tended with soft incantations,
Some had juleps to drink,
Or round about their limbs he laid his simples,
And for some the knife: so he set all up straight.

Yet even Wisdom
Is in bondage to gain. Him too
55 A princely wage seduced, when the gold
Gleamed in his hand,
To raise from the dead
A man whom death had taken.
But Kronos' son
Cast with his hands at the two of them:

Quickly he tore the breath out of their breasts
And the blazing thunderbolt drove death home.
– We must ask from the Gods
Things suited to hearts that shall die,
60 Knowing the path we are in, the nature of our doom.

Dear soul of mine, for immortal days
Trouble not: the help that is to be had
Drain to the last. And yet, if only
Wise Cheiron were still living in his cave,
And the honey of our songs laid a spell on his soul,
65 O surely I had moved him to send, even now,
One that should heal good men
From burning sicknesses,
One called Son of Latoïdas or of the Father.
I would have ploughed the Ionian Sea
And come by ship to the Fountain of Arethoisa,
To my friend of Aitna town;

IV

70 Who reigns in Syracuse
A King, kind to his people, not envying merit,
To strangers a marvellous father.
Could I have landed with double delight for him,
With a golden gift of health,
And a triumph to make bright the Pythian crowns,
Which Pherenikos the conqueror horse
Won at the games
In Krisa once –
75 No star in heaven, I say, had then shone farther
Than I, as I came from crossing the deep sea.

But I wish to make my vow to the Mother.
To her and Pan the Maidens sing

97

Before my house,
Goddess of awe, in the nights.
80 And you, Hieron,
Having the wit to know
What sayings are sharp and true, have learned the old
        proverb:
'With every blessing God gives a pair of curses.'
This is what fools cannot bear with decency;
But good men can, and turn the fair part outwards.

Your portion of Felicity attends you.
85 On the Prince who rules his people, if on any,
Is the eye of mighty Fate,
        Untroubled life.
Neither Peleus had, the son of Aiakos,
Nor godlike Kadmos.
These two, they say, had the utmost bliss of men:
They heard the Muses
90 Singing, with gold in their hair,
On that mountain and in seven-gated Thebes
(When one
Married soft-eyed Harmonia, and one Thetis,
Wise Nereus' golden child)

V

And with both the Gods feasted. They saw those Kings,
The sons of Kronos, sitting on golden thrones,
And took their marriage-gifts.
95 Through the favour of Zeus, they put from them
Their former sorrows, and set their hearts up straight.
– But time passed on: and from Kadmos
Three of his daughters, by their sharp anguish,
Took away his share of delight,
– Though father Zeus came to the lovely bed

98

Of white-armed Thyona –

100 And Peleus' son, the only son
Whom immortal Thetis bore to him in Phthia,
Killed by an arrow in battle, was burned with fire
And woke the Danaans' tears.
   If any man understands the way of truth,
When the Blessed Ones send him aught,
He must needs be happy.
105 Many are the high-flying winds, and blow many ways:
Man's bliss does not go steady for long
When it follows him with all its weight.

I will be little when little is my circumstance
And great when it is great. What doom,
Now or to come, attends me,
By that I shall set my heart, and serve it after my
   measure.
110 If God should give me the luxury of wealth,
I think surely I should know
Thenceforth the heights of fame.
   Of Nestor and the Lykian Sarpedon,
Those household names,
The loud lines speak, which craftsmen built with skill,
And thence we know them.
Greatness in noble songs
115 Endures through time: but to win this, few find easy.

Pythian III, written about 474 B.C., is not an Epinician but a poetical epistle to Hieron, who is ill and has asked Pindar to visit him in Sicily. Pindar, with some elaboration, refuses.

1–60 The double myth of Koronis and her child, Asklapios, illustrates the danger of trying to pass beyond the proper limits for men, and enforces Pindar's advice that Hieron should not indulge too strong hopes of recovery.

8 The daughter of Phlegyas is Koronis, who, when with child by Apollo, promises to marry Ischys.

26 The stranger is Ischys.

28 In earlier versions Apollo heard the news from a raven.

32 Apollo sends Artemis to kill the guilty couple.

45 The child, Asklapios, is given to Cheiron to be educated.

54 Asklapios is bribed to raise a man from the dead, and is punished for it.

61 Pindar addresses himself, but what he says is more relevant to Hieron.

74 The horse Pherenikos is celebrated in *Olympian I*.

77 Pindar explains that he cannot come to Syracuse because he is busy with the cult of Pan and the Great Mother (Kybele). This would be taken seriously.

110 Pindar suggests that he would like a handsome reward, but leaves it not very explicit. It is possible that this was prompted by the large fine inflicted on him by the Thebans for praising Athens.

NEMEAN III

For Aristokleidas of Aigina, winner in the
trial of strength

I

Lady Muse, our mother, I beg you,
Come in the holy Nemean month
To Aigina's welcoming Dorian island.
By Asopos' water young men are waiting,
5 Craftsmen of honey-toned songs, in desire of your
voice.
Everything done thirsts for one thing or other,
But victory in the Games loves song most of all,
Most deft attendant on wreaths and on prowess.

Give it without stint from my skill,
10 And begin, daughter of the sky's many-clouded King,
A hymn of glory. I shall partner it
With their choir and the lute.
Its task shall be pleasant,
To be a jewel on the land
Where of old the Myrmidons dwelt.
Their company, ancient in story,
15 Aristokleidas has not fouled with reproaches
– Such was your will – nor did he turn soft

In the brawny ranks of the Trial of Strength.
For wearying blows in Nemea's deep plain
He brings a health-giving cure in victory's prize.
If Aristophanes' son, being beautiful,
Has done what befits his beauty
20 And scaled the heights of manhood,

Yet to travel further is not easy
Over the untrodden sea beyond the Pillars of Herakles.

II

Them the god-hero placed to witness to all
Of the limit of sailing.
He broke monstrous beasts in the sea
And alone tracked the currents in the shallows,
25 Till he came to the bounds which send men home,
And made the earth known.
　My heart, to what stranger cape
Do you turn my voyage?
I bid you bring the Muse to Aiakos and his race;
High Justice wafts the saying: 'Praise the noble.'

30 Nor are desires for what is not his
Better load for a man. Make your search at home.
You have found the ornament you deserve,
A sweet song to sing. In tales of old prowess
Is that of King Peleus' joy.
He cut an enormous spearshaft,
And single-handed, without an army,
Took Iolkos, and caught
35 The sea-maiden Thetis by might and main.
Stalwart, strong Telamon
Destroyed Laomedon, with Iolas at his side.

He followed him in pursuit
Of the brawny bronze-bowed Amazons,
Nor did terror that breaks a man
Dull the edge of his spirit.
40 (A man has much weight if glory belongs to his breed,
But whoso needs to be taught,
His spirit blows here and there in the dark,

Nor ever enters he the lists with sure foot,
Though countless the glories his futile fancy savours.)

III

Brown-haired Achilles stayed in Philyra's home,
A child whose play was mighty exploits.
Often his hands threw
45 The short iron javelin to rival the winds;
He dealt death in battle to ravening lions
And boars were his prey. Their panting bodies
He brought to the Centaur, Kronos' son,
In his sixth year at first, then through all his days.
50 Artemis marvelled at him, and bold Athana,

That he killed deer without hounds or treacherous
traps.
By his feet he defeated them. (What I tell
Was spoken by men of old.)
Deep-counselling Cheiron
Nursed Jason inside his stone dwelling,
And Asklapios after him,
55 And taught him the use of medicine with gentle hands.
In time he found a wedding
For Nereus' bright-bosomed daughter;
He cherished her noble son for her, and exalted
His spirit in all things fitting,

That, sent by the sea-winds' blasts to Troy,
60 He should stand up to the clash of spears and the battle-
cry
Of Lykians and Phrygians and Dardanians,
And fight hand to hand with Ethiopian spearmen,
And nail to his heart the resolve
That their sultan, Helenos' mad-hearted kinsman,
Memnon, should not come back home.

IV

From him is the light of the Aiakidai
Firm-fixed, a beacon flame.
65   Zeus, thine is their blood and thine the struggle
Which my song has struck,
As in young men's voices it cries aloud the land's delight.
The clamour is right for the victor Aristokleidas,
Who has set this island on words of glory,
And on bright hopes of honour
70   The holy Hall of the Pythian God.
Trial reveals the end in which each man surpasses,

Among boys a boy, a man among men,
And among elders, thirdly –
In each state that belongs to our mortal breed
75   Man's life drives a four-in-hand of excellences
And bids us give thought to what lies in front.
These he lacks not. Greeting, my friend!
I send you this honey mixed with white milk,
And mingling dew is spread on it,
A drink of song on the breath of Aeolian pipes,

80   Late though it be. The eagle is swift among birds,
And with a long sweep from afar
Suddenly seizes the bloody prey with its talons,
While the chattering daws range low.
For you, now that that bright-throne Kleio is willing,
Because of your victorious spirit
From Nemea and from Epidauros
And Megara light looks out.

Nemean III was composed about 474 B.C., but there was an interval
between the victory celebrated and the actual celebration (80).

3 The Aiginetans prided themselves on their Dorian origin.

10 The Muse, daughter of Zeus, must begin the song, but Pindar is the intermediary between her and the choir.

13 The Myrmidons are the first inhabitants of Aigina, and their name was thought to be connected with *murmekes*, 'ants', which, according to legend, were changed into men.

22-6 After introducing the theme of Herakles, Pindar leaves it. Its purpose is to set the right standard for heroic performance, but Herakles is not an Aiginetan; so Pindar moves to local heroes.

33-6 Peleus normally gets his spear from Cheiron; here he cuts it for himself. Normally, too, he does not take Iolkos without help from others. Pindar stresses his unique strength.

36-9 Telamon takes Troy in the first siege.

40-42 Pindar puts forward his doctrine that mere teaching will not make an athlete or a soldier or a poet; he must have an inborn gift.

43-63 A myth of Achilles, especially of his childhood, when he was taught by the Centaur Cheiron.

54 Other pupils of Cheiron are Jason and Asklapios.

65 The victor's family claims descent from Zeus.

70 In Aigina there was a temple of Apollo used by his special interpreters.

70-75 There are three ages of man – youth, maturity, and old age. In each the four traditional virtues, wisdom, justice, reverence, and temperance, must be applied to the right conditions at the time.

76-80 In remarkable imagery Pindar indicates the sweetness and lightness of his song.

80 Pindar is like an eagle catching his prey – in catching his theme. The daws are his imitators who scavenge his leavings.

83 Kleio, later the Muse of history, is still a Muse of song.

OLYMPIAN X

*For Hagesidamos of Western Lokroi, winner in
the boys' boxing*

I

Read me the name of the Olympian victor,
Archestratos' son –
Where in my heart is it written?
I had forgotten I owe him
A sweet song. But, Muse,
And you also, Truth, daughter of Zeus,
5   Keep off with uplifted hand
The lying reproach
That I have done wrong to a friend.

From far away the future
Has come upon me and made me ashamed
Of my deep debt.
Yet interest has power
To deliver me from wounding complaints.
10   See how the flowing wave
Now drowns the rolling shingle
And how we shall carry out our contract
To his dear delight.

For Simplicity rules the city
Of the Lokrians in the West,
15   And their care is for Kalliopa
And brazen Ares.
– Even prodigious Herakles
Was routed in battle with Kyknos –.
Let Hagesidamos,
Who has won in the boxing at Olympia,

Thank Ilas as Patroklos thanked Achilles.
20 One born to prowess
May be whetted and stirred
To win huge glory
If a God be his helper.

II

Without labour few find joy,
A light upon life that makes up for all efforts.
The ordinances of Zeus have roused me
To sing of the grandest of Games,
Which by the ancient tomb of Pelops,
25 With contests six in number, Herakles founded
When he slew Poseidon's son, fine Kteatos,

And slew Eurytos, to exact
From violent Augeas,
Willing from an unwilling giver,
The wages for his serfdom.
30 In bushes under Kleonai
He trapped and broke them on the road;
For his Tirynthian army,
When it sat in the vales of Elis,
Had been slaughtered before

By the insolent Moliones;
35 The Epeians' king, cheater of strangers,
Soon afterwards saw his rich land in stubborn flame,
And under strokes of iron
Into a deep pit of doom
His own city sinking.
40 (There is no way to put aside
The struggle against the stronger.)
And he last of all, in his folly,
Met capture and escaped not precipitous death.

III

The strong son of Zeus drove the whole of his host
And all his booty to Pisa,
45 And measured a holy place
For his mighty Father.
He fenced the Altis and marked it off
In a clean space, and the ground encircling it
He set for rest at supper,
In honour of the Ford of Alpheos

And the twelve Kings of the Gods.
50 To Kronos' Hill he gave a name; for before
It was nameless when Oinomaos ruled,
And drenched with many a snowstorm.
In this first birthday-rite
The Fates stood near at hand,
And he who alone proves the very truth,

55 Time. In his forward march
He has revealed all clearly:
How Herakles portioned the booty, war's gift,
Made sacrifice and founded
The fourth year's feast
With the first Olympiad
And the winning of victories.
   Who won the new crown
60 With hands, feet or chariot,
Set in his thoughts a prayer for the struggle
And got it in deed?

IV

In the foot-race the best
65 Was Oionos, Likymnios' son, who ran
A straight stretch on his feet;

He came from Midea pressing his company.
In wrestling, Echemos brought honour to Tegea,
And Doryklos won the prize for boxing,
A dweller in Tiryns city.
In the four-horsed chariot

70 Samos won, Halirrothios' son
From Mantinea. With the javelin,
Phrastor hit the mark, and Nikeus,
Circling his hand with a stone,
Threw it far beyond all.
His fellow-fighters
Flashed into a loud uproar.
The evening was lit
75 By the lovely light of the fair-faced moon.

All the holy place was loud with song
In the glad feasting like the music of banquets.
   We follow the first beginnings
And in the namesake song of glorious triumph
We shall sing aloud of the thunderbolt
80 And the fire-flung shaft of Zeus, the noise-awakener,
The flaming lightning, fitting in every victory;
The luxuriant music of songs
Shall answer the pipe.

V

85 Late indeed have they appeared
By glorious Dirka;
But as the son of his wife, long desired,
Is to a father come to youth's opposite,
And warms his heart exceedingly with love;
(For wealth that gets for shepherd
A stranger from an alien house

90 Is most hateful to a dying man),

So when a man has done well unsung,
Hagesidamos, and comes to death's threshold,
He has breathed to no purpose, and won
Small delight by his labour.
But on you delight is shed
By the sweet-voiced harp and the pleasant flute.
95 Your far-flung glory is in the charge
Of the Pierian Maidens, daughters of Zeus.

I lend my hand to them eagerly. I have embraced
The Lokrians' famous people;
I drench with my honey
Their city of noble men.
100 I have praised the loved son of Archestratos,
Whom I saw winning with valour of hand
By the Olympian altar in those days,
Beautiful in body
And touched by the youthfulness
Which once kept shameless death away
105 From Ganymedes, with help of the Kypros-born.

*Olympian X was composed in fulfilment of a promise given in Olympian
XI 4–5, but after some delay – about 474 B.C.*

13 Lokroi was governed by laws given by the famous law-giver
Zaleukos.

14 It has a local tradition of poetry, especially of love-songs.

15–16 In his fight with Kyknos Herakles was at first defeated, but
returned to the attack and won. The abrupt allusion may hint that the
victor here looked like losing but won all the same.

17 The victor should give thanks to his trainer Ilas.

24–57 The origin of the Olympian Games. Herakles cleansed the stables
of Augeas, but Augeas refused to pay his fee. Herakles proceeded to
lead an army against him, but was attacked by Poseidon's sons, Kteatos
and Eurytos.

34 The Epeians' king is Augeas.

43 ff. Herakles marks out the ground for his new Games – called the Altis – and builds twelve altars for the chief Gods.

49 The Hill of Kronos is on the edge of the Altis.

51 It is not clear why in the time of Oinomaos (see *Olympian I*) there was snow at Olympia.

52 The Fates are present as at a birth-day.

64–75 The first Olympian Games. The winners are for the most part unknown, and Pindar seems to have followed some poem of local interest, possibly composed in Argos in the seventh century.

NEMEAN IV

For Timasarchos of Aigina, winner in the boys' wrestling

I

Joy is the best healer
Of labours decided, and Songs,
The Muses' wise daughters,
Charm her forth by their touch,
Nor does warm water so drench and soften the limbs
5 As praise joined to the harp.
Longer than actions lives the word,
Whatsoever, with the Graces' help,
The tongue picks out from the depths of the mind.

II

Such may it be mine to offer
To Zeus Kronidas and to Nemea
10 And to Timasarchos' wrestling
In prelude to my hymn.
May the tall-towered home of the Aiakids welcome it,
A beacon for all in its goodness to strangers.
If your father Timokritos
Were still warmed by the strength-giving sun,
He would often have swept the cunning harp
15 With this song to support him,
And have renowned his son, the glorious victor,

III

Who has sent a necklace of wreaths from the games at
Kleonai

And from glittering, fortunate Athens;
And because in seven-gated Thebes
By Amphiaraos' famous tomb
20 The Kadmeians were not sorry to cover him with flowers
For Aigina's sake.
Loving he comes to those that love him,
And lets his eyes fall on a friendly city
Towards Herakles' happy hall.

IV

25 With him strong Telamon once spoiled Troy and the
    Meropes,
And the huge warrior, horrible Alkyoneus, –
But not before he had broken
Twelve four-horse-teams with a rock
And heroes, tamers of horses, riding upon them,
30 Twice the number.
Ignorant of battle would that man be plainly
Who understands not my words;
What is done must be paid back in kind.

V

I am kept from telling the whole long tale
By the rules of song and the hurrying hours;
35 But magic pulls at my heart
To touch on the new moon's feast.
Nevertheless, though the deep salt sea
Holds you by the waist, strain against its stratagems.
When we come to the struggle in the light of day
We shall be seen far to outdo our enemies;
While another with envious eyes
40 Rocks in the dark his unballasted thought

VI

And runs it aground. Whatever prowess
King Fate has given to me,
I know well that oncoming time
Will accomplish what has to be.
Weave, sweet harp, at once
45   In Lydian melody
This song also, loved by the Vineland and Kypros,
Where Telamon's son, Teukros, reigns apart,
While Aias keeps his father's Salamis,

VII

And Achilles a shining island in the Friendly Sea.
50   Thetis reigns in Phthia, and Neoptolemos
On the limitless mainland,
Where tall headlands of cow-pasture
Start from Dodona to slope the Ionian Strait.
By the foot of Pelion Peleus assaulted Iolkos
With deadly thrust
55   And gave it to the Haimonians in bondage;

VIII

He knew the crafty tricks
Of Akastos' wife, Hippolyta.
With the dagger of Daidalos
60   Pelias' son was planting death for him from an ambush.
But Cheiron protected him
And carried out the predestined fate of Zeus.
Peleus baffled all-powerful fire,
Sharp claws of bold cunning lions
And the edge of their terrible teeth,

IX

65 And wedded one of the high-throned Nereids.
   He saw the fine seats in a circle
   Where the Kings of Sky and of Earth
   Took their places and showed favours
   And power to his race.
   To the darkness beyond Gadeira
   No one may pass;
   Turn back the ship's tackle
70 To the mainland of Europe.
   I cannot go through the whole tale of Aiakos' sons.

X

I have come from the Theandridai,
Prompt with news of the struggles
In which their thews were braced
75 At Olympia and the Isthmos and Nemea;
I keep my bargain.
There they were put to the test
And came not home without garlands whose fruit is
   glory
To the land, Timasarchos, which your clan serves
With triumph-songs that ring in our ears.
80 If you bid me set up to Kallikles, your mother's brother,

XI

A monument whiter than Parian marble,
Gold in the testing shows all its brightnesses,
And song in praise of fine doings
Makes a man equal in fortune to kings.
85 May he who dwells by Acheron hear my voice echo,
   Where in the Games of the loud Trident-lifter
   He was green with Korinthian parsley.

XII

Him gladly would Euphanes, his father's old father,
90 Have sung to his cronies.
Every age has its companions,
But each man believes that he can tell best
What he himself has encountered.
How, in his praise of Melesias,
He would twist in the fight, make his words come to
grips,
Not to be thrown in his speech as he grapples,
95 Gentle of heart to the noble
But grim as he lies in ambush for his foes.

Nemean IV was written about 473 B.C. for a victory won not at Nemea
but in the Games of Adrastos at Sikyon.

12 'the tall-towered home' is Aigina.

13 If the victor's father were alive he would accompany this song with
his harp.

16–20 Timasarchos has won prizes at the Nemean Games (Kleonai),
Athens, and Thebes.

25–30 The first Trojan War.

36–8 Pindar suggests that his journey to Aigina has difficulties, notably
among men who are envious of him, but he will surmount them.

46–54 Pindar names various Aiakidai and their realms.

56 ff. A short reference to Peleus and Hippolyta as in *Nemean V*.

62–5 Thetis took the form of various wild animals which Peleus had to
subdue before he could marry her.

65 The Gods attended the wedding of Peleus and Thetis.

69 Gadeira (Gades) marks the end of the known world.

80 Kallikles is uncle of Timasarchos. Pindar's song takes the place of a
marble memorial to him.

89 Euphanes is grandfather of Timasarchos.

93 Melesias is a famous Athenian trainer.

NEMEAN IX

For Chromios of Aitna, winner in the chariot-race

I

Muses, our revel shall come from Apollo at Sikyon
To newly built Aitna,
Where guests have overwhelmed the wide-flung doors
Of Chromios' happy home.
Come, shape words into a sweet melody.
For he mounts his team of victorious horses
And gives the sign for a song
In honour of the Mother and her twin children
5 Who share and watch over precipitous Pytho.

II

There is a saying of men: 'Hide not
On the ground in silence a noble thing done.'
Come, we shall wake the thundering harp and the flute
For the top of horse-races,
Which, in honour of Phoibos, Adrastos
First held by the streams of Asopos.
I shall name it
10 And clothe with echoing glories the hero,

III

Who was king there in those days
And renowned and revealed his city
With new feasts and the struggles of men
In strength and carved chariots.
Once he fled from the bold plotter Amphiaraos,

From the fearful strife in his father's house and from
    Argos.
Talaos' sons no longer ruled;
Sedition had broken them;
15 – The stronger man ends the right that was before.

IV

Eriphyla, breaker of men,
They gave as a pledge under oath to the son of Oikleës,
And were the mightiest of the fair-haired Danaoi.
Time was when to seven-gated Thebes
They led an army of soldiers
On a road where the portents were against them.
Kronos' Son brandished his lightning
To urge them not to press their mad march from home
20 But to hold back from the journey.

V

Into stark destruction
The host hurtled on its way,
With armour of bronze and horses' accoutrements.
On the banks of Ismenos
They were robbed of their sweet home-coming
And with their bodies they fattened the white flowers of
    smoke.
Seven pyres feasted on young men's limbs,
But Zeus with his all-powerful thunderbolt
Split the earth's deep breast for Amphiaraos
25 And hid him with his horses,

VI

Before he, a soldier, could be stabbed in the back
By Periklymenos' spear to the shame of his heart;

For when fear comes from the Gods
Even their sons run away.
    If it may be, son of Kronos,
I put away as far as I can
This fierce ordeal for life or death
Against spears flung by the Phoenicians,
And ask Thee to grant for long years
The gift of good government
30 To the sons of Aitna's men,

VII

Father Zeus, and to shed on the people
Glories that honour the city.
Men live there who are lovers of horses,
And have hearts above possessions.
I say what is past belief;
For Shamefastness who brings honour
Is secretly tricked by gain.
If you carried Chromios' shield
Among fighters on foot and horses and battles at sea,
35 You would have seen in the hazard of the shrill battle-cry

VIII

How that Goddess stiffened his warrior-spirit in fight
To keep off the War-God's ruin.
Few have power and skill in hand and soul
To turn back from their feet the cloud of slaughter
Against the ranks of the foe.
Yet they say that the glory of Hektor flowers
By the floods of Skamandros;
40 And above the sheer cliffs of Heloros' coasts,

IX

At the place called Area's Ford, for Hagesidamos' son
This light shone in the beginning of manhood.
I shall tell of his doings on other days,
Many on dusty land, some on the neighbouring sea.
From labours done with youth and with right
Comes a life of calm until old age.
Let him know that he has won
45   A wonderful fortune from the Gods.

X

For though a man has great riches
And wins an illustrious name,
He is mortal and may travel no further
To set his foot on another goal.
Peace loves the feast, and with soft song
Victory bursts into fresh flowers;
And the voice grows bold by the mixing-bowl.
50   Mix it, the sweet inspirer of revelry,

XI

And deal out the vine's strong child
In the silver cups
Which once his mares won for Chromios
And sent to him from holy Sikyon
With garlands woven by Right, from Lato's Son.
Father Zeus, I pray to make loud this prowess
With the Graces to help me,
And may my words surpass many in honouring victory
55   As I shoot straight at the Muses' mark.

Nemean IX was composed about 473 B.C. for a victory won not at
Nemea but at the Games of Adrastos at Sikyon.

2 Chromios had been appointed by Hieron to be governor of the new town of Aitna, where the song is to be sung.

4 The Mother and her twin children are Lato, Artemis, and Apollo.

9 The Games at Sikyon were believed to have been founded by Adrastos. That is why Pindar tells of the Seven against Thebes, of whom Adrastos was one.

13 Early in life Adrastos fled from Argos to Sikyon.

16 Eriphyla, sister of Adrastos, was given in marriage to Amphiaraos, son of Oikleës.

19 ff. The expedition failed completely. Five of the seven leaders were killed; Amphiaraos was swallowed up in the earth, and only Adrastos came home safely.

28 Pindar refers to the wars of the Akragantines against the Carthaginian invaders of Sicily, and perhaps suggests that the latter have been defeated because they have not respected the Gods.

34 Chromios has fought in these battles.

41 The Ford of Area has not been identified, but it is where Gelon, Hieron's brother, won the victory which gave him the mastery of Syracuse.

OLYMPIAN VI

For Hagesias of Syracuse, winner with the mule-car

I

We shall set golden pillars
Under the chamber's well-made porch
And build, as it were, a marvellous hall;
When work is begun,
The front must be made to shine afar.
    If there were an Olympian victor,
5   Steward at Pisa of God's oracular altar,
And founder's kin to glorious Syracuse,
What hymn would that man not have
If he found his townsmen
Unstinting in songs that he loves?

Let the son of Sostratos know
That to this sandal the Gods have fitted his foot.
Success without risk is not honoured
10 Among men or in hollow ships;
But if a fine task is done,
Many remember it.
Hagesias, the praise waits for you,
Which Adrastos spoke
In justice from truthful lips
For the son of Oikleës, Amphiaraos,
When the earth swallowed him and his shining mares.

15 Then, when the seven pyres of the dead were done,
Talaos' son spoke such a word in Thebes:
'I pine for the eye of my army,
Twice excellent,

Prophet and champion with the spear.'
This word holds of a man,
The Syracusan master of the victory-choir.
I am not out to quarrel
Nor over-eager to win,
20 But I shall swear a mighty oath and witness
This for him truly,
And the honey-tongued Muses will approve.

II

Come, Phintis, now yoke the strong mules for me
Quickly, that in a clean road
We may mount the car and I may come
25 To a race of true men.
Beyond others these mules know
To lead the way; for they have won
Wreaths at Olympia. Therefore to them
I must fling wide the gates of song
And come in good time today
To the ford of Eurotas and to Pitana.

She wedded, story tells
30 Kronos' son, Poseidon,
And bore the violet-haired girl, Evadna.
She hid her maiden travail in her dress,
And in the month of birth she sent servants
And told them to give the child to Eilatidas' keeping –
He ruled at Phaisana
Over the men of Arkadia,
And had Alpheos for home;
35 There Apollo cared for her, and first
She touched the delights of Aphrodita.

All that time she hid her child by the god,
But kept not her secret from Aipytos.

With carking care he beat down
Unspeakable wrath in his heart
And went on his way to Pytho
To ask about the sorrows he could not bear.
She laid down her belt of scarlet woof
40 And her silver pitcher under a blue bush,
And bore a child of godlike spirit. To her
The Golden-Haired sent
The kind-hearted Birth-Goddess and the Fates.

III

From her womb and from the loved travail
Came Iamos straight to the light.
45 In sharp distress she left him on the ground,
But the Gods planned
That two bright-eyed serpents
Should nurse and feed him
On the innocent poison of bees.
When the King came driving from rocky Pytho,
He questioned all in the house
On the child whom Evadna had borne:
'The boy is begotten of Phoibos

50 For sire. He shall surpass all men
In prophecy to dwellers on earth,
And his race shall never fail.'
So spake he, and they swore
They had not seen or heard of the child,
Though he was five days old. He was hidden
In the reeds and the pathless briars,
His delicate body soaked
55 With gillyflower rays of yellow and deep purple.
Therefore his mother proclaimed
That for all time he should be called

By this undying name.
When he plucked the flower of youth
The delightful, the golden-crowned,
He went down to the middle of Alpheos
And called on Poseidon, the wide ruler,
His grandfather, and on the Archer,
The Watcher of Delos, built by the Gods.
60 He asked for himself the honour of nursing his people,
At night under the sky.
Clear-toned his father's words
Spoke in answer and called him:
'Rise, son, and behind my voice
Come hither to a land which all shall share.'

IV

They came to the steep rock
65 Of Kronos' exalted son, who gave him there
A double treasure of prophecy:
'Now you shall hear a voice that knows not lies,
And when Herakles, the bold deviser, comes,
A holy shoot from Alkaios' sons,
And founds a feast of many men
For his Father and orders the greatest of Games,
70 You shall set up an oracle
On the topmost altar of Zeus.'

Since then the breed of Iamos' sons
Has wide renown among the Hellenes.
Prosperity went with them.
They honour achievement and pass
To a way for all to see.
Their witness is each thing done.
Abuse from envious rivals
Hangs over all

75 Who drive in first on the twelfth round,
   While a holy Grace
   Sheds honour and beauty upon them.
   If in truth, Hagesias, the men of your mother's race
   Dwelt under Kyllana's boundaries

   And honoured often in humbleness
   With many a suppliant sacrifice
   The Gods' Messenger, Hermes,
   Who has charge of the Games and the allotting of prizes,
80 And honours Arkadia and its brave men, he,
   Son of Sostratos, with his loud-thundering Father
   Brings your good luck to fulfilment.
       On my tongue I feel
   A sharp whetstone, and all willing
   I am dragged towards her with lovely streams of song
   By my mother's mother,
   Stymphalian Metopa,
   With beautiful flowers.

V

   Her daughter was Theba, the driver of horses,
   Whose beloved water I shall drink
   When I weave my patterned song for fighting men.
       Now stir your companions, Aineas,
   First to proclaim aloud Hera of the Maidens,
   And then to know if in honest truth we are quit
90 Of the old gibe 'Boiotian pig'.
   For you are a trustworthy messenger,
   Cipher-stick of the lovely haired Muses,
   Sweet mixing-bowl of loud-sounding songs.

   I have told you to remember Syracuse
   And Ortygia, which Hieron rules

With a clean sceptre and justice in his heart.
95 He cares for crimson-footed Damater and for the feast
Of her daughter, the white-horsed lady,
And for the strength of Zeus of Aitna.
The sweet-voiced harps and songs know him.
May coming time not shatter his bliss.
But with that gentleness men love
May he welcome the victory-choir of Hagesias,

When it comes from one home to another,
From the walls of Stymphalos,
100 Leaving Arkadia's mother and her fine flocks.
On a winter's night it is good
To have dropped two anchors from a swift ship. May
    God
Love them and bestow
Fortune and fame on both races.
    King, Lord of the Sea,
Give straight sailing out of trouble,
O husband of golden-spindled Amphitrita,
105 And swell to fruit the delicious flower of my songs.

Olympian VI was written in 472 B.C. and performed at Pitana in
Arkadia by a choir which Pindar had instructed, though he was not
present at the performance.

4–7 Hagesias, son of Sostratos, comes from an ancient, founding
family at Syracuse, and is also a seer who interprets burnt offerings at
Olympia.

12 Hagesias is compared with Amphiaraos for being both a soldier and
a seer.

13 When Amphiaraos is swallowed up in the earth before Thebes,
Adrastos praises him for his double gifts.

22 Phintis is the charioteer of Hagesias, and drove the victorious mule-
car, which is now imagined as driving through the air to Pitana.

29–70 Myth of Iamos, an ancestor of Hagesias, and founder of a famous
clan.

29–30 Pitana sleeps with Poseidon and bears the child Evadna.

35 Evadna sleeps with Apollo and has the child Iamos, whose birth is told at length. Her father is Aipytos, son of Elatos.

47 The 'poison of bees' is honey. Pindar plays with the verbal echo in Iamos of the word *ios* meaning 'poison', as he does also in 55 with the word for gillyflowers, *ia*.

58 Second stage of the myth – Iamos and Apollo.

84 ff. Pindar finds a connexion between himself and the victor's home, because Theba is the child of the Stymphalian Metopa.

88 Aineas is the choir-master.

89 In performing the song he will show that the Boiotians do not deserve their name of 'pig' for rural crudity.

91 A cipher-stick was for sending cryptic messages, since the message wrapped round the stick could be read only by someone who had a stick of exactly the same shape.

99 ff. Hagesias has a second home in Syracuse, where he is a friend of Hieron.

OLYMPIAN XII

For Ergoteles of Himera, winner in the long foot-race

I beg you, daughter of Zeus the Deliverer,
Watch over Himera's wide dominion,
Saviour Fortune. At your will
Fast ships are steered on the sea,
5 And on land stormy wars and assemblies at council.
The hopes of men are now thrown up,
Now down again, as they cleave
The wind-tossed sea of lies.

No man on earth has yet found from the Gods
A certain token of success to come,
But their sight is blinded to what is to be.
10 Many things fall against men's reckoning,
Contrary to delight, and others,
After facing the enemy surges,
Exchange in a brief moment
Sorrow for deep joy.

Son of Philanor, in truth like a cock in the yard
The fame of your running would have shed its leaves
15 Ingloriously by your kinsmen's hearth,
Had not the quarrel of men with men
Robbed you of your Knossian fatherland.
Now, being crowned at Olympia,
And twice from Pytho, and at the Isthmos,
Ergoteles, you exalt the Nymphs' hot springs
Dwelling by fields your own.

Olympian XII was written in 470 B.C.

1–2 There had recently been a revolution in Himera, and Pindar prays that things may turn out for the best.

13–16 Ergoteles is by birth a Cretan from Knossos, but civil strife has sent him to Sicily.

19 Himera was famous for its hot springs.

PYTHIAN I

For Hieron of Aitna, winner in the chariot-race

I

O lyre of gold, Apollo's
Treasure, shared with the violet-wreathed Muses,
The light foot hears you, and the brightness begins:
Your notes compel the singer
When to lead out the dance
The prelude is sounded on your trembling strings.
5 You quench the warrior Thunderbolt's everlasting
     flame:
On the eagle of Zeus the eagle sleeps,
Drooping his swift wings on either side,

The king of birds.
You have poured a cloud on his beak and head,
And darkened his face:
His eyelids are shut with a sweet seal.
He sleeps, his lithe back ripples:
10 Your quivering song has conquered him.
Even Ares the violent
Leaves aside his harsh and pointed spears
And comforts his heart in drowsiness.
Your shafts enchant the souls even of the Gods
Through the wisdom of Lato's son
And the deep-bosomed Muses.

And things that Zeus loves not
Hear the voice of the maids of Pieria: they shudder
On earth and in the furious sea.
15 And *he* is afraid who lies in the horrors of Hell,

The Gods' enemy,
Typhos the hundred-headed,
Nursed once in the famed Cilician Cave.
But now above Kyma the foam-fronting heights,
And the land of Sicily, lie
Heavily on his shaggy chest.
The Pillar of Heaven holds him fast,
20 White Aitna, which all the year round
Suckles its biting snows.

II

Pure founts of unapproachable fire
Belch from its depths.
In the day-time its rivers
Pour forth a glowing stream of smoke:
But in the darkness red flame rolls
And into the deep level sea
Throws the rocks roaring.
25 And that huge worm
Spouts dreadful fountains of flame –
A marvel and wonder to see it, a marvel even
To hear, from those that are there,

What a monster is held down
Under Aitna's dark-leaved peaks, and under the plain.
The bed he lies on
Driving furrows up and down his back
Goads him.
                    Let, O Zeus,
Let thy favour be found, thou that art on
30 This mount, the brow of a fertile land.
Whose namesake city near
Took her great founder's glory: the herald declared it
On the course at Pytho, when he cried the name

'Hieron!', proud victor

In the chariot-race. – Sea-faring men
Look first for the luck of the wind
To start them outward: they reckon
35 That promises well for the road home at the end:
So does this happy fortune
Give argument to hope
That this city shall have renown for ever
For wreaths and horses,
And fame in the music of her feasts.
   Thou Lykian, thou Lord of Delos,
Phoibos, who lovest
Kastalia, Parnassos' stream,
40 Be pleased to have this in thy thought
And enrich the land with men.

III

For the Gods give all the means of mortal greatness.
They grant men skill,
Might of hand and eloquence.
My praise is ripe for One:
I do not mean
To make a No-Throw with the javelin's bronze cheek
That quivers in my hand,
45 But with a great cast to outdistance all the field.
Ah! may the rest of time guide him straight
As now, in prosperous and rich possession,
And grant him to forget his troubles.

Then will he remember the wars and the battles,
When his soul endured, and he stood firm,
When in the strength of the Gods his house won glory
More than is reaped by any in Hellas,
50 A nobleness to crown their wealth.

– But this last time he went to war
Like Philoktetes of old: (enforcement here
Brought even a mighty Lord
To fawn on him for friendship).
For the godlike heroes fetched from Lemnos once
(The tale says), weary with his wound,

The son of Poias, the archer:
Who broke down Priam's city and ended the Danaans'
    toil,
His body weak as he went, yet it was foreordained.
    So God be Hieron's maintainer
In the time that comes, and give him
Enough of his heart's desire.
    Muse, I pray you consent
To sing in the house of Deinomenes also
The chariot's due of song:
He too has joy in his father's victory.
Come, now, let us find a song
Of love for Aitna's King.

IV

Hieron founded for him this city
In the Gods' pattern of freedom.
He founded her in the laws
Which the people of Hyllos keep;
A race born of Pamphylos,
Yes, and of the sons of Herakles,
That dwells below the heights of Taygetos,
Has chosen to remain for ever in the Laws of Aigimios
A Dorian people. They prospered and took Amyklai;
From Mount Pindos they came.
Now beside the Tyndaridai, the lord of white horses,
They dwell deep in glory:

The renown of their spears has come to flower.

God the achiever,
I pray that by the waters of Amenas
A fate like this may be set aside for ever
For the men of the city and their princes,
By the truthful speech of men.
With thy help, the man who leads them
70 (And he shall instruct his son)
Shall give his people honour, and turn them
To peaceful concord. – Grant, I beg,
O son of Kronos, that the Phoenician
And the Tyrrhenians' war-cry
Keep quiet at home: it has seen what woe to its ships
Came of its pride before Kyma,

And all that befell when the Lord of Syracuse routed
    them,
Who out of their swift-sailing ships
Cast down their youth in the sea
75 – The dragger of Hellas from her weight of slavery.
    Salamis shall win me
The thanks of the Athenians for payment;
And in Sparta the battles before Kithairon,
For there the Medes gave way with their bended bows:
But by Himera's well-watered banks
A song composed for Deinomenes' sons,
That their valour earned
When the hosts of their enemies gave way.

V

Say enough and no more,
And spin in a slender twine
The threads of many tales,

And men shall carp less at your heels.
Tedious Too-much dulls the quick edge of hope:
And words in a city weigh on men's hidden pride
Worst, when you say good things of another.
85   Yet, to be envied is better than pitied!
Loose not your hold on beautiful things.
Guide your host with a rudder of justice,
And on an anvil of truth
Forge an iron tongue.

Any small spark struck out,
Being yours, flies with power.
Disposer of many,
Many are the witnesses and true
Of your good and evil.
Abide in the fair garden of your spirit,
90 And, if you love to be always in pleasant report,
Like a helmsman let out the sail to the wind.
Never believe, dear friend, in the close fist's cunning:
Only the glory of fame which they leave behind them

Proclaims men's way of life, when they die,
In history and in song.
The excellent kind heart of Kroisos does not perish,
95 But the pitiless soul,
That roasted men in his bull of brass,
Phalaris, in every land
His evil fame overwhelms him.
No harps call him into the hall,
Blending softly his name
With the voices of boys.
Good fortune is the best and first of prizes,
Good name the second possession:
100 The man who has found both and keeps them
Has won the highest crown.

Pythian I was written in 470 B.C. and performed in Sicily at the celebrations for Hieron's new city of Aitna, on the former site of Katana.

1–12 Music on Olympos is a counterpart to the music on earth at the present festival.

15–20 Typhos, the Giant, fought the gods and was buried under Aitna.

18 Kyma, on the west coast of Italy, near Naples.

21–8 The eruption of Aitna took place in 474 B.C., and in that case Pindar did not see it.

29 Pindar turns to Hieron's achievements, with special reference to the new town of Aitna.

51 Hieron suffers from the stone and yet went to battle at Kyma in 474 B.C. He is compared with Philoktetes, who, despite a diseased foot, went to Troy and played a leading part in its capture.

58 Deinomenes, young son of Hieron, is titular King of Aitna.

61–5 Aitna is to be a city on the Dorian model, as established by Hyllos, son of Herakles.

72 The Phoenicians (Carthaginians) and the Tyrrhenians (Etruscans) were routed by Hieron in the battle of Kyma.

75–8 Hieron's victory puts him on a level with the Athenians for winning the battle of Salamis, and the Spartans that of Plataea.

94 Kroisos, king of Lydia, was regarded as a model of piety because of the rich gifts he gave to Apollo at Delphoi.

95–6 Phalaris, tyrant of Akragas in the middle years of the sixth century, was said to have roasted his victims in a brass bull.

ISTHMIAN II

For Xenokrates of Akragas, winner in the chariot-race

I

The men of old, Thrasyboulos,
To the harp's loud accompaniment
Mounted the gold-ribboned Muses' chariot,
And gaily shot honey-toned songs at boys,
At any who, being beautiful, had
The sweetest summer
5   That woos Aphrodita on her noble throne.

For the Muse then was not yet greedy for gain
Nor worked for pay,
Nor did the sweet-voiced songs of Terpsichora
Silver their faces and ply for hire.
But now she bids remember the Argive's saying
10   That comes near to the very truth:

'Money, money makyth man,' he said,
When he lost his possessions and friends together,
– Well, you are wise. I sing a victory
Not unknown, won by horses at the Isthmos,
Which Poseidon granted to Xenokrates,
15   And sent him to bind on his hair
A wreath of Dorian parsley.

II

He honoured a fine charioteer, a light of the men of
    Akragas.
In Krisa also the wide ruler Apollo beheld him
And gave him glory;

20 In radiant Athens
   He won the favouring fame of Erechtheus' sons,
   And had no cause to blame the hand of a man
   Who whipped up his horses and looked after his chariot.

   This hand Nikomachos gave to all the reins
   In the right nick of time;
   Him the heralds of the seasons knew,
   The Eleans, who keep the truce of Zeus, son of Kronos;
   For they had enjoyed what he did in kindness to strangers,
25 With sweet-breathed voice they greeted him
   When he fell at the knees of golden victory

   In their own land, which they call
   The holy place of Olympian Zeus.
   There the sons of Ainesidamos are joined
   To unperishing honours.
30 Not unacquainted are your halls, Thrasyboulos,
   Either with loved revelry
   Or with sweet-swelling songs.

III

   No hill is there, nor is the way steep,
   If one of the Daughters of Helikon
   Brings honour to the home of far-famed men.
35 May I make a long throw with a quoit
   And shoot so far
   As Xenokrates surpassed all men in sweetness of mood;
   Modest was he in speech with his townsmen,

   And took thought of horse-breeding
   In the manner of all the Hellenes.
   He opened his arms to every feast of the Gods;
   Nor ever at his generous table
40 Did a gale blow and lower his sail;

But in summer he passed to the Phasis,
And in winter he sailed to the shore of Nile.

Therefore because jealous hopes
Hang round the hearts of men,
Let his son not be silent on his father's prowess,
45   Or on these songs; for I
Have not made them to stand idle.
Give these to him, Nikasippos,
When you come to my honoured friend.

Isthmian II is not an Epinician ode but a poetical epistle sent by Pindar to his old friend Thrasyboulos (see *Pythian VI*) through Nikasippos, presumably a common friend. The date may be about 470 B.C. when Xenokrates and Theron were both dead, and the latter's rule had been overthrown. Pindar seems to be asking for money in a roundabout way on the plea that in the past he wrote a song for Xenokrates and was not paid for it.

1 ff. Pindar seems to have some words of Anakreon in mind and may be thinking of the love-poetry written by Anakreon and others of his time.

6 Simonides was said to be the first poet to take money for his songs, but before him Arion made a fortune in Sicily and Italy.

7 Terpsichora is a Muse.

9 ff. The Argive is a man called Aristodemos, of whom nothing is known but this remark.

21 Erechtheus is the legendary ancestor of the Athenians.

22 Nikomachos was the charioteer of Xenokrates.

24 The Eleans looked after the Olympian Games, which could be attended in time of war by visitors from all parts of Greece.

28 The sons of Ainesidamos are Theron and Xenokrates.

41-2 The metaphorical language indicates the scope of Xenokrates' hospitality.

43 The words indicate the political confusion in Akragas in the years after Theron's death.

ISTHMIAN I

For Herodotos of Thebes, winner in the chariot-race

I

Mother of mine, golden-shielded Theba,
I shall set your task above all occupation.
Let not rocky Delos, in whom I have poured my heart,
Be angry with me.
5 What do the good love more than honoured parents?
Give place, Apollo's island. With the Gods' help
I shall join these two delights and fulfil them,

As I sing of Phoibos the long-haired God,
With men of the sea in wave-girt Keos,
And of the Isthmos rock that breasts the foam;
10 For from its Games it has given
Six garlands to the host of Kadmos,
A fame of fine victory to our land.
There did Alkmana bear her undaunted son,

Before whom Geryon's dogs once shuddered.
  But I fashion for Herodotos
A gift for his four-horsed chariot,
15 And since he handled its reins with his own hands,
I wish to fit him into a song
Fit for Kastor or Iolaos.
In Lakedaimon and Thebes they were born,
Strongest of heroes in the driving of chariots.

II

In the Games they put their hands
To many encounters

And made their home fine with tripods,
20 With cauldrons and cups of gold;
They relished the wreathes that victory brings.
The light of their success is manifest
In the naked foot-races and in the running
Of warriors in clanging armour,

When their hands aimed sharp spears,
25 And when they went among the stone quoits.
There was no Five Events, but each exploit
Had an end of its own.
Often, their hair bound with many garlands from these,
They were seen near to the streams
Of Dirka and to Eurotas.

30 Iphikles' son was born of the same breed
As the Sown Men, and Tyndareos' son
Dwelt among the Achaians
On the high seat of Therapna.
Hail to you! But I will deck a song
For Poseidon and the holy Isthmos
And the shore of Onchestos
And proclaim in the tale of this man's honours
The glorious lot of his father Asopodoros,

III

35 And his father's fields in Orchomenos,
Which welcomed him from the immeasurable sea
When he was cast ashore by shipwreck
In freezing misfortune;
But now the destiny of his blood
40 Has set him again in the bright daylight of old.
He who has suffered gains foresight with his mind.

If he gives all his spirit to prowess,

Both with expense of money and with toil,
To those who have found it we should pay
A proud song of praise with ungrudging temper.
45 For this is a light gift for a craftsman to make
In return for troubles of every kind –
To speak a fair word and set up
A fine sight for all to see.

After action different rewards
Delight different men,
Sheep-watcher, ploughman, snarer of birds,
And him whom the sea feeds.
But every man strains in effort to keep
Nagging hunger away from his belly.
50 But he who in games or in war
Wins delicate glory,
Gets the highest gain in words of praise,
The best that the tongues of townsmen and strangers can
 utter.

IV

We must raise a loud song for our neighbour,
The Earth-shaking Son of Kronos,
And thank him for helping our chariots,
Lord of the horse-races.
55 And your sons, Amphitryon,
We must greet, and the home of Minyas,
And Eleusis, the famous grove of Damater,
And Euboia in the circling running-grounds.

Protesilas, with these I count
Your precinct among Achaian men at Phylaka.
60 From telling everything
That Hermes, God of the Games,
Has given to Herodotos with his horses.

I am stopped by the brief scope of my song.
Truly what is kept in silence
Brings even larger delight.

May it be his lot to be borne aloft
On the shining wings
65 Of the sweet-voiced Pierian maidens,
And wreathe his hand with the choicest garlands
From Pytho and the Olympiads at Alpheos,
As he fashions honour for seven-gated Thebes.
But if anyone dispenses hidden wealth indoors,
And laughs when he falls on men unlike himself,
He thinks not that he pays his life
To death ingloriously.

Isthmian I was written about 470 B.C.

2 Pindar ought to be composing a Paean for the men of Keos, to be sung at Delos, but postpones it to write *Isthmian I*. Remains of the Paean survive as *Paean IV*.

13 The mere appearance of Herakles frightened the fabulous dogs of the monster Geryon. The words are meant to give a brief hint of how formidable Herakles was.

15 Unlike many other patrons of chariot-racing, Herodotos drives his own chariot, and is therefore compared with Kastor and Iolaos, who also did.

26 In early days there were separate prizes for wrestling, running, jumping, discus, and javelin, which later made up the Five Events.

30 Iphikles' son is grandson of Amphitryon and Alkmana, and nephew to Herakles.

32 Tyndareos' son is Kastor.

35 The family of Herodotos has been living at Orchomenos. The shipwreck is presumably metaphorical, connected with the exile of Herodotos after the Persian War. He has now returned to Thebes.

55 The sons of Amphitryon are Herakles and Iphikles, in whose honour games were held at Thebes.

56 ff. Various places where Herodotos has won prizes.

59 Protesilas was killed at the very beginning of the Trojan War. There was a cult of him at Phylaka in Thessaly.

67–8 The end of the poem sketches someone who is the antithesis of Herodotos. He does not spend his money and does not see how inglorious his life is.

PYTHIAN II

For Hieron of Syracuse

I

Mighty City of Syracuse!
Where Ares dwells in depths of war,
Where men and horses mailed for battle
Have holy nurture, to you I come
Bringing from shining Thebes this song. I tell
5 How, where the teams of four horses made earth tremble,
Hieron and his good chariot conquered
And wreathed Ortygia with far-shining crowns,
Where the Lady of Rivers, Artemis, dwells.
She failed him not
When with light hand on the embroidered reins
He broke those young mares in.

For she, archeress maiden, with either hand,
10 And Hermes, Lord of the Games,
Put on the bright harness, when to the smooth car
And the axle that follows the rein
He yokes the strong mares,
And calls on the Trident-lifter, the far-felt God.
   For one or another king a poet makes
The clear-voiced hymn, the due of his greatness.
Often in Kypros they celebrate with song
15 Kinyras, whom Apollo the golden-haired
Delighted to love,

And Aphrodita stalled him in her temple.
Their songs are of thanks and worship
For the labours of his love.

But your name, O son of Deinomenes,
The girl of Lokris-in-the-West
Sings on her doorstep: after the toils and despairs of war
20 Because of your strength her eyes are steadfast.
   They say that Ixion, commanded by the Gods,
Speaks thus to man, on his winged wheel turning all
      ways:
'Thou shalt be zealous for him that does thee service
And pay him gentle return.'

II

25 He learned that surely. Among Kronos' kindly sons
Lapped in sweet ease, he stayed not long in bliss,
Fool in his wits!
Who loved Hera, her that is set apart
For the mighty joys of Zeus. But pride drove him
To blind presumptuous folly.
30 He suffered soon his due, getting a choice award of woe.
His two sins live and bring him misery: one
That he, a hero, first and with guile
Brought kindred blood upon men,

The other that in the great darkness of a bridal chamber
He tempted the wife of Zeus.
(Let a man, when he measures,
Remember his own size!) His lawless love
35 Cast him into great depths of evil
When he came to her bed: for he lay by the side of a
      Cloud,
Clasping a sweet lie, ignorant man.
Its shape was like the most mighty daughter of Kronos
The son of Heaven.
40 The hands of Zeus made it,
To snare him, a lovely sorrow.

And so, bound to the four spokes,

He got his own ruin.
Thrown in fetters he shall not escape, he proclaims
His universal message.
Far were the Graces when the Cloud
Bore him a monstrous issue,
She like nothing, and like nothing It;
Which found no favour among men, nor in
The company of the Gods.
She nursed It and called It Kentauros: and It lay
45 With the Magnesian mares on Pelion's foot-hills.
And a race was born
Prodigious, in the image of both parents,
Their nether parts of the mother, their father's above.

III

God reaches, as soon as thought, his ends:
50 God, who can catch the winged eagle
And overtakes the dolphin in the sea.
He can bring down any whose heart is high,
And to others he will give unaging splendour.
But I
Must keep from the sharp bites of slander:
For far in the past I see
55 Archilochos the scold in poverty,
Fattening his leanness with hate and heavy words.
Wealth, and the fortune
To be wise as well, is best.

And that, men see, is yours.
Your free heart displays it,
Sovran master of the many streets
Which crown your city, and of a host of men.
And if anyone says

That riches like that and such great glory
60 Were ever yet surpassed by the older Hellenes,
The fond fool struggles in vain.
I will climb to the flowery bows
And make noise of your greatness.
Youth asks for courage in the terrors of war:
And thence you won
Your infinite renown.

65 Fighting now in the charging cavalry,
Now with the men on foot.
Your riper age's wisdom
Gives me a theme, where without peril I sound
The whole gamut of praise.
   Good-bye. This song
I am sending, like a Phoenician merchant, over the grey
     sea.
And on the Kastoreion's Aeolian mood, so please you,
Look: turn to it, if ever
70 You liked my seven-stringed harp.
O find, and be, yourself! 'O that
Lovely ape!' cry the children, 'O how

IV

Lovely!' But Rhadamanthys has found bliss,
Because his judgement bore him fruit without cavil,
And his heart in him has no pleasure in lies,
75 The constant retinue of crafty whispering men.
– Whom you cannot fight, and they spoil two lives,
Sly hinters of slander,
Their minds exceedingly like foxes' minds.
   Yet Lady Vixen was not so cunning for once –
Let the rest of the tackle toil in the sea's depth, I
80 Am the cork that rides the surge. I'll get no ducking!

He cannot throw his word like a man
In honest company, your twisting knave –
He fawns upon all, weaving fine threads of mischief.
My boldness is not his. Let me love my friend,
But if I must fight my foe, I'll be wolf and make for his
    legs,
85 I'll be here and there, and twist and turn!
And yet, whoever governs, way is made
For the straight-spoken man;
Where one is king, or when a city is overwatched
By the brute multitude, or by the wise.
No man must fight with God,

Who exalts now those, then to others anon
He will give great splendour. But that
90 Is little comfort for envious minds.
They strain at a course they cannot stay,
And the sharp wound is in their heart, or ever
Their careful schemes come right.
Let them take the yoke on their neck
And bear it lightly: it were best.
95 To kick against the goads is the way
To come sprawling. – May I have the regard
Of the noble, and be with them.

Pythian II, like Pythian III and Isthmian II, is not a true Epinician but a poetical letter, sent probably in 468 B.C. to Hieron who has just won the chariot-race at Olympia and asked not Pindar but Bacchylides to celebrate it. Pindar attributes this rebuff to slanderers at Hieron's Court and, while protesting his admiration and affection for Hieron, lets himself go in denouncing these sycophants.

3 Pindar writes the poem in Thebes and sends it to Syracuse.

4–8 To win the chariot-race at Olympia was regarded as the highest possible success.

9 The 'archeress maiden' is Artemis.

12 The 'Trident-lifter' is Poseidon.

15 Kinyras is mentioned as an example of a man whom the Gods love. He was a priest-king at Paphos in Kypros and loved alike by Apollo and Aphrodite.

18–20 Hieron has recently saved Western Lokris from Kroton.

31–2 Ixion killed his father-in-law, Eioneus, but was forgiven by the Gods.

21–48 Myth of Ixion, on the theme of ingratitude. Pindar seems to indicate with what horror he regards it and so disclaims being guilty of it. We may also detect a latent hint that Hieron is more likely to be guilty of ingratitude than Pindar.

33–4 Ixion assaults Hera, but a cloud takes her place, from which (42 ff.) a monstrous being, Kentauros, is born. From this and the mares on Pelion are born the Centaurs. Kentauros is Pindar's own invention, intended to soften the violence of the Centaurs' origin.

53 ff. Pindar does not wish to be accused of having a sharp tongue, and quotes the sad precedent of Archilochos, a poet of the early seventh century, who was renowned for his savage quarrels.

68 The song sent by Pindar 'like a Phoenician merchant' comes, as it were, on approval, to remind Hieron of what kind of poet Pindar is.

69 Pindar asks Hieron to look at some earlier song that he has written for him.

72 Hieron must be his true self on the lines of the Delphic motto 'Know thyself'.

72 The sudden break in the tone and sequence indicates the degree of Pindar's resentment. The ancient commentators say that the ape is Bacchylides, who wrote his *Ode V* for this occasion and certainly imitates Pindar in what might be thought an ape-like way.

73 Against the slanderers Pindar sets Rhadamanthys, judge of the dead, as the ideal of fairness and honesty.

78 The slanderers do themselves no good, and Pindar is untouched by them.

86 Pindar will speak his mind freely, no matter what the form of government is.

90 The slanderers again. It is not quite clear in what pursuit they hurt themselves, and the point of the words is that in Greek 'strain' and 'wound' echo the same sound.

OLYMPIAN IX

For Epharmostos of Opous, winner in the wrestling

I

Archilochos' tune that rang at Olympia,
The threefold, loud song of victory,
Was enough to guide to Kronos' Hill
Epharmostos in triumph with his own companions;
5 But now from the long-range Muses' bow
Sweep with arrows like these
Zeus of the scarlet thunderbolt
And Elis' holy peak,
Which of old the Lydian hero, Pelops,
10 Won as Hippodameia's most beautiful dowry,

And shoot a sweet feathered arrow at Pytho.
The words you handle
Will not fall to the ground,
When you make the harp strings tremble
For a man's wrestling, who comes
From glorious Opous. Praise herself and her son;
15 She belongs to Right
And her daughter great in glory,
Saviour Lawfulness.
She flowers in acts of prowess
By your stream, Kastalia, and by Alpheos.
Thence the pick of all garlands exalts in glory
20 The Lokrians' mother among her shining trees.

On that dear city
I kindle light with flaming songs,
25 And faster than thoroughbred horse or ship on the wing

I shall send this news to every quarter,
If by fate's device I dwell
In a choice garden of the Graces.
They give delightful things, but 'tis their destinies
That makes men noble and wise.

II

For how could Herakles
30 Have brandished a club in his hands against the trident,
When Poseidon stood over Pylos and drove on him,
And Phoibos drove, shaking his silver bow?
Nor did Death keep the rod unshaken
With which he brings down
35 The bodies of men to the hollow street of the dying?
Fling this tale away, my lips!
For to revile the Gods is an odious art,
And to boast beyond measure

Is a tune for the song of madness.
40 Babble not now of such things. Put aside
Every battle and war of Immortals.
    Lend your tongue to Protogeneia's town,
Where Zeus of the flashing thunderbolt decreed
That Pyrrha and Deukalion
Should come down from Parnassos
And set their first home. Without wedlock
45 They made a single race
Of a generation of stones:
They were called People.
Awake for them the liquid path of words;
Praise an old wine, but the blossoms of songs

That are new. They say that the power
50 Of waters flooded the black earth,

But Zeus planned that an ebb
Should suddenly check the tide. From them
Were your brazen-shielded ancestors
Begotten in the beginning, children
55 Of the daughters of Iapetos' stock
And Kronos' mighty sons,
Kings in the land for ever,

III

Until the prince of Olympos
Plucked Opous' daughter from the Epeians' land
And slept with her secretly
In the Mainalian Hills
And brought her to Lokros,
60 Lest the years overtake him
With the doom of a childless breed.
But his bride held the mightiest seed, and the hero
Was pleased when he saw the son she brought him,
And named him after his mother's father,
65 A man surpassing in beauty and action.
He gave him the people and city to govern.

To him came strangers
From Argos and Thebes, Arkadians and Pisatans also,
But above all newcomers he honoured
Menoitios, Aktor's child and Aigina's,
70 Whose son went with the Atreidai to Teuthras' plain
And stood with Achilles
Alone, when Telephos routed the strong Danaoi
And fell on the sea-going prows.
He taught wise men to learn
75 Of Patroklos' valiant heart.
Then Thetis' son begged him
Never in murderous war

To take a post far away
From his own man-conquering spear.
80   May I find words to lead others
And be fit to ride in the Muses' chariot.
May daring and power follow me in abundance.
By his prowess and office I come
To champion Lampromachos' crowns at the Isthmos,
Since both are conquerors

IV

85   In their task on a single day.
Twice again was the joy of victory theirs
In the gates of Korinth,
And for Epharmostos in Nemea's valley.
At Argos he won fame among men,
And as a boy at Athens;
And what a fight he put up at Marathon,
90   When dragged away from the striplings,
With older men for the silver cups.
In his fast crafty twists
He slipped not but beat down his rivals,
But to what cheers he went round the ring,
Being young and beautiful,
And most beautiful what he had done.

95   Then to the Parrhasian people
His marvels were made known
At the feast of Zeus Lykaios.
At Pellana he won the warm remedy against cold winds.
Iolaos' tomb is witness,
And Eleusis by the sea, to his glory.
100 What nature gives is in every way best, but many
Have tried to win renown
By taking lessons in prowess.

If a God is not there, nothing
Is worse for being kept in silence, for some roads

105   Go farther than others. No single training
Will look after all of us.
All skills are steep, but bring this prize
And boldly roar aloud
110   That by divine will this man has been born
Strong of hand, lithe of limb,
With valour in his eyes,
And by his victory, Aias Ileus' son,
In your feast he has crowned our altar.

Olympian IX was written in 466 B.C. and sung at the victor's home in Opous, two years after his Olympian victory.

1–4 At the actual time of victory at Olympia Epharmostos had to be content with the simple victory-song attributed to Archilochos in which the main feature was the three times repeated refrain.

9–10 The story touched upon is told in *Olympian I*.

11–12 Epharmostos won the wrestling at the Pythian Games in 466 B.C. and this would be fresh news when the poem was composed.

29–40 Pindar rejects stories that Herakles fought against the Gods.

41–79 The myth falls into two parts, (i) the flood which destroyed the first race of men, except for Deukalion and Pyrrha, who created a new race; (ii) the origins of Patroklos, the friend of Achilles.

41 Protogeneia is the daughter of Deukalion and Pyrrha and the ancestress of the new race of men.

46 Pindar plays on the words *las*, 'stone', and *laos*, 'people'.

53 The ancestors of Epharmostos were kings of Lokris, and descended from Zeus and Kambysa (58).

58 The daughter of Opous is Kambysa, or a second Protogeneia.

70 The son of Menoitios is Patroklos.

71 Teuthras and Telephos (72) were kings of Mysia.

84 Epharmostos' brother won in the Isthmian Games on the same day as Epharmostos in the Olympian.

85–99 A list of Epharmostos' victories.

89 At Marathon he seems to have been taken forcibly from the boys and made to compete with the mature men.

97 The 'warm remedy' was a woollen garment.

100 Pindar states his usual belief in breeding.

112 The ceremony takes place at the altar of the younger Aias.

NEMEAN VII

For Sogenes of Aigina, winner in the boys' five events

I

Eleithyia, seated at the side
Of the deep-thoughted Fates,
Daughter of strong and mighty Hera, listen,
Bringer of children to birth.
Without you we see not the day or the black night,
Nor find your sister, bright-limbed Youth.
5 But not for like ends do we all draw breath;
As many as men are the different destinies
That yoke each to his doom and hold him.
By your help Thearion's son,
Sogenes, has been proved in valour,
And song proclaims him victorious
Among winners of the Five Events.

– He dwells in the song-loving city
10 Of the Aiakidai, the spear-strikers.
They are glad to look after
A heart well trained in the struggle.
If any man's actions prosper, he strikes
A honey-hearted well of the Muses' streams.
Even high deeds of bravery
Have a great darkness if they lack song;
We can hold a mirror to fine doings
In one way only,
15 If with the help of Memory in her glittering crown
Recompense is found for labour
In echoing words of song.

Wise sailors have learned
Of the wind that comes on the third day,
And lust for profit brings them to no harm.
The rich man and poor man together
20 Come to death's boundary.
But I hold that the name of Odysseus
Is more than his sufferings
Because of Homer's sweet singing;

II

For on his untruths and winged cunning
A majesty lies.
Art beguiles and cheats with its tales,
And often the heart of the human herd is blind.
25 If it could have seen the truth,
Aias would not, in wrath about armour,
Have driven a smooth sword through his breast.
After Achilles he was the strongest in battle
Of all who were sent in fast ships
To fetch his wife for brown-haired Menelaos
By the speeding breath of the straight West Wind

30 To Ilos' city. To all comes
The wave of death and falls unforeseen
Even on him who foresees it.
But honour grows for the dead
Whose tender repute a God fosters.
One came, a Champion,
To the great navel of broad-bosomed earth,
– In the floor of Pytho he lies –
35 Neoptolemos. He sacked Troy's city,
Where the Danaoi also toiled.
He sailed away and missed Skyros;
In their wanderings they came to Ephyra.

For a little time he was king in Molossia,
40 And his race always holds this honour.
He went to the God with wealth from the loot of Troy,
And there he fell in a fight
Over a victim's flesh,
And a man struck him with his sword.

III

His Delphian hosts were exceedingly grieved at it,
But he paid what was foreordained.
It was doomed that one of the royal Aiakidai
45 Should stay for ever within the ancient place
By the God's well-walled house;
He should remain and see right conduct
Of the heroes' processions and multitudinous sacrifices.
For honour and justice three words shall suffice:
No lying witness, Aigina,
50 Watches over the doings
Of sons sprung from you and Zeus.
I make bold to say this –

For shining successes
The royal road of words begins at home.
Yet in every task a pause is sweet;
Even honey cloys,
And Aphrodita's delicious flowers.
Each of us differs in blood
And has a separate life;
55 One man has this, and one that.
No man can have the luck to win good fortune entire.
I cannot tell
To whom Fate has given this end for certain.
But to you, Thearion, she grants
A right moment of happiness:
In you who have found daring to do well

60 She spoils not the mind's understanding.
   I am a guest. I keep black reproach away.
   I shall bring true glory like running water
   To the man that I love, and praise him.
   This reward is right for the noble.

IV

   If a man of Achaia be near
65 In his home above the Ionian Sea,
   He will find no fault with me.
   I am host to his city and trust in that.
   Among my own people the look is clear in my eyes.
   I have not overshot the mark; I have thrust
   All violence from my goings.
   May the rest of my days come to me with kindness.
   Any who knows me can tell
   If I come with a song that is harsh and out of tune.
70 Sogenes, son of the Euxenid race, I swear
   That I did not step over the tape
   When I shot my quick tongue

   Like a bronze-cheeked javelin
   Which frees neck and thews from the sweat of wrestling
   Before limbs fall into the glaring sunlight.
75 Let me be. If in exaltation
   I raised too loud a cry,
   I am not sour about paying a song of joy to the victor.
   To plait garlands is easy. Strike up! The Muse
   Welds together gold and white ivory
   And the lily-flower snatched from the sea's dew.

   Remember Zeus, and for Nemea
80 Swell softly the many-toned range of song.
   On this ground it is right to sing
   With gentle voice of the King of Gods.

For he, they say, planted the seed of Aiakos
In his mother's welcoming womb,

V

85 To rule towns in his own lucky land,
And to be your loyal friend and brother, Herakles.
If a man finds delight in a man,
We can say that neighbour to neighbour,
Should he love with unfaltering heart,
Is a joy worth everything.
If God too gives support to this,
90 With you who broke the Giants to help him,
Sogenes will be glad to live in good fortune
And nurse a heart kind to his father
In his ancestors' rich and holy road.

As between the yokes of a four-horsed chariot
He has his home in your precincts
On either hand as he goes.
You, Blessed One,
95 Must win Hera's Lord and the bright-eyed Maiden;
You can often give succour to men
From the maze of confusion.
May you link days of enduring strength
To his youth and happy age,
And weave them for him in bliss.
100 May his children's children for ever

Have what today gives and better hereafter.
My heart shall never say
That I have savaged Neoptolemos
With dishonouring words. To plough
Three times and four the same field
105 Is futility, like one idly yapping
To children of 'God's own Korinth'.

Nemean VII seems to have been written about 467 B.C. A little earlier is
Paean VI, of which fragments survive, and which was sung at Delphoi.
Pindar had given offence to the Aiginetans by his frank account of their
hero Neoptolemos, who had killed Priam and was buried at Delphoi
after being killed in a brawl there. *Nemean VII* combines the theme of
the boy's victory and appropriate sentiments of the relation of song to
glory with the theme of Neoptolemos, on which Pindar makes some
small concessions but no apology.

12–16 Song keeps the memory of great doings alive.

17–30 Song gives some men more than their due (Odysseus) and some
less (Aias).

30 The mention of Troy provides a point of transition to Neoptolemos,
who is buried at Delphoi and stays there as a protecting hero.

35 Pindar substitutes this vague phrase for the explicit statement in the
Paean that Neoptolemos 'killed old Priam, when he flung himself on the
altar of the hearth'.

38–9 Nothing is now said about the unsuccessful character of Neopto-
lemos' reign in Molossia.

42 The death now comes from an unknown man 'with a knife'
instead of from Apollo. Also the fight is now simply 'about meats'
instead of over the rights of the priests.

44 ff. It is part of the divine plan that Neoptolemos should stay after
death within the precinct of Apollo.

49 The witness is Neoptolemos.

50 ff. Pindar returns to the theme of the victor.

75 A slight hint of the Neoptolemos theme.

77 Anyone can compose a song, but not such a song as Pindar com-
poses.

79 'The lily-flower' is coral.

83 ff. Herakles and the Aiakidai are praised.

92 ff. The house of Sogenes lies between two shrines of Herakles, like
the pole of a four-horsed chariot between the double yoke.

102–5 Pindar reverts for the last time to Neoptolemos.

105 'God's own Korinth' was a proverbial example of boring repeti-
tion, perhaps connected with a children's game.

OLYMPIAN VII

For Diagoras of Rhodes, winner in the boxing

I

As a man takes in his rich hand a bowl
Bubbling inside with the wine's dew,
And shall give it
To his daughter's young bridegroom to pledge him
From one home to another,
– All of gold, crown of possessions,
5 Joy of the revel, – and honours his bridal,
And makes him to be envied before his dear ones
For his wedding in which two hearts are one,

So I too pass flowing nectar,
The Muses' gift, sweet fruit of the heart,
To men who win prizes,
And make them glad,
10 To winners at Olympia and Pytho. Happy is he
Who is held in good report.
Beauty, who gives strength to life,
Turns her eyes now on this man, now on that,
With the harp often and the flute's music in every key.

With both I have landed
In Diagoras' company, chanting
The sea-maiden, Aphrodita's child
And the Sun's bride, Rhodes,
15 That I may praise a straight fighter, a towering man,
Crowned at Alpheos for his boxing, and at Kastalia,
And his father Damagetos, who gives pleasure to Right;
On a three-towned island,

With the ship's beak of broad Asia for neighbour,
They dwell among Argive spears.

II

20 For them I have a message
And wish to set straight from the start,
From Tlapolemos, a tale that belongs to all the race
Of Herakles, whose strength spreads far;
For on their father's side they boast themselves
From Zeus; through their mother,
Astydameia, they are sons of Amyntor.
About the wits of men hang faults past number,
25 And there is no way to discover

What now and in the end is best
For a man to get. For once
At Tiryns the founder of this land
In anger slew with a hard olive-staff
Alkmana's brother, Likymnios,
30 When he came from Midea's chambers,
(The heart's confusions send even a wise man astray.)
He went to the God and questioned his oracle.

From his sweet-scented shrine the Golden-Haired
Told him to sail straight from Lerna's shore
To a sea-girt pasturage, where of old
The great King of the Gods
Soaked a city in golden snowflakes,
35 When, by the craft of Hephaistos
And his bronze-beaten axe, from the top of her Father's
      head
Athana jumped out, and cried with a monstrous shout,
And the sky shuddered at her, and Mother Earth.

III

Then the God who gives light to men,
40 Hyperion's child, bade his loved sons
Look to their coming task, be first to build
A manifest altar for the Goddess,
Make holy sacrifices, and rejoice
The Father's heart, and the Daughter's, the lightning-
         speared.
(If forethought is honoured,
It casts prowess and joy among men;

45 But past calculation comes a cloud
Of forgetfulness and drags the straight path of duty
Away from the mind.)
They went up without the seed of flaming fire,
And with sacrifices unburnt
Made a holy place on the mountain-top.
Zeus gathered for them a tawny cloud
50 And rained much gold, and the Bright-Eyed One gave
         to them

Every craft, to surpass earth-dwellers
In hands most skilful at labour.
Streets carried their works like to living
Creatures and walking: and deep was their glory.
(In skilful hands art is better without guile.)
55   The ancient tales of men report
That when Zeus and the Undying Ones portioned the
         earth,
Rhodes was not yet to be seen in the sea's water,
But an island was hidden in the salty depths.

IV

The Sun was away, and no lot was declared for him;
They left him without a portion of Earth,

60 A God undefiled.
 When he spoke of it, Zeus was for ordering
 A second cast, but the Sun forbade;
 For he said that in the grey sea
 He saw swelling up from the bottom
 A land with much food for men and friendly to flocks.

 Straightway he told gold-veiled Lachesis
65 To lift her hands and not betray
 The great oath of the Gods,
 But, with Kronos' son, to grant
 That, when it was sent to the bright air,
 It should be his special gift henceforward.
 The high words fell out in truth
 And were fulfilled. There grew
 From the sea's salt brine

70 An island. It belongs
 To the father and master of piercing sunbeams,
 The lord of fire-breathing horses.
 There on a day he wedded Rhodes, and begat
 Seven sons, who inherited wisdom
 Beyond all earlier men.
 Of them one begat Kamiros,
 And Ialysos for firstborn,
75 And Lindos. They portioned their father's land
 In three, and kept their separate share of cities,
 And their places are called by their names.

V

 A sweet requital for his pitiful fortune
 Is set up to Tlapolemos, the captain from Tiryns,
 As to a God,
80 And the strong reek of the flocks' procession,
 And trial in the Games.

In their flowers Diagoras was twice crowned;
At the famous Isthmus he was four times fortunate,
And in this victory after that
At Nemea, and in hollow Athens.

The brazen shield at Argos knew him, and the prizes
In Arkadia and Thebes, and the games
85 Of the Boiotian land, and Pellana.
Six times he won at Aigina, and at Megara
The stone record holds no other tale.
    Father Zeus, ruler on Atabyrion's ridges,
Honour the rite of Olympian victory,

And a man who has found prowess in boxing.
Grant him favour and joy
90 From citizens and from strangers.
For he goes straight on a road that hates pride,
And knows well what a true heart
From noble fathers has revealed to him.
Hide not any who shares in the seed of Kallianax.
When the Eratidai rejoice, the city also
Is feasting. In a single moment of time
95 Many are the winds that blow this way and that.

Olympian VII was composed in 464 B.C. and performed at Rhodes.
In later times the poem was inscribed in golden letters at Lindos. The
family of Diagoras was famous both for athletic prowess and for
political activity on the anti-democratic side.

1–10 Pindar compares his song with a pledge made in a golden bowl
for a wedding.

13 This suggests that Pindar himself has come to Rhodes. The nymph,
Rhodes, is the child of Aphrodita and the Sun.

15 Diagoras has won the boxing in the Olympian and the Pythian
Games.

17 The city of Rhodes was not built until the fourth century. The three
ancient cities were Kamiros, Ialysos, and Lindos.

19 The first colonists came from Argos with Tlapolemos.

20–38 The first myth – Tlapolemos and the founding of Rhodes. It illustrates how a wrong action can yet lead to a good result.

27 We do not know why Tlapolemos struck Likymnios.

34 The golden rain on Rhodes is an expansion of a line of Homer, *Iliad II, 670.*

35–8 Pindar makes this coincide with the birth of Athana from the head of Zeus, as depicted on the eastern pediment of the Parthenon.

45 ff. The second myth – the inauguration of fireless sacrifices on Mount Atabyrion. Here too a mistake – forgetfulness – leads to a happy conclusion. The Bright-Eyed one is Athana.

52 ff. Pindar refers to the early Rhodian artists. He does not mention by name the Telchines, because they had a name for undue cunning, but suggests an improved version of them.

54–69 The birth of Rhodes from the sea. Here too a mistake leads to a good result.

71 ff. Grandsons of the Sun and Rhodes are the three eponymous heroes of the Rhodian cities Kamiros, Ialysos, and Lindos.

81–7 The athletic victories of Diagoras.

93 The Eratidai, to whom Diagoras belongs, are descended from Kallianax, a Heraklid.

94–5 It is tempting to see some political reference in these last lines, but the metaphor is common in Pindar and may refer to no more than the sudden emergence into fame of Diagoras and his family.

OLYMPIAN XIII

*For Xenophon of Korinth, winner in the foot-race
and the five events*

I

Three times an Olympian victor
Is the house I shall praise,
Gentle to townsmen, of service to strangers.
I shall come to know fortunate Korinth,
5   Poseidon's porch on the Isthmos,
Glorious in its young men.
There Lawfulness dwells, and her sisters,
Safe foundation of cities,
Justice, and Peace, who was bred with her;
They dispense wealth to men,
Golden daughters of wise-counselling Right.

They wish to keep away
10   Pride, the bold-spoken mother of Surfeit.
    I have fine things to say, and upstanding courage
Stirs my tongue to speak.
(The way of the blood is hard to fight or to hide.)
Many times, sons of Alatas,
Has the brightness of victory been given to you
15   From men who surpass on the heights of success
In the holy Games,
And many wise devices of old
Were set in the hearts of men

By the flower-laden Hours.
Each thing belongs to its finder.
Whence came the delights of Dionysos

20 With the ox-driving Dithyramb?
Who added the bridle to horses' harness?
Or the king of birds
Fore and aft on the God's temples?
There the Muse breathes sweetly; there Ares flowers
Among young men's deadly spears.

II

O mightiest One, ruler afar of Olympia,
25 Be not grudging to our prayers
For the whole of time, father Zeus.
Guide this people out of harm
And give a straight wind to Xenophon's fortune.
Welcome from him this rite of crowns and choir,
Which he brings from the plain of Pisa,
30 Victor in the foot-race and the Five Events together;
He has won what no mortal man has won before.

Two wreaths of wild celery crowned him
When he showed himself
At the Isthmian Games, and Nemea
Does not resist him.
By Alpheos' stream is dedicated
35 The glint of foot of his father Thessalos;
And at Pytho he has the glory
Of the foot-race and the double-race in a single sun;
And in the same moon at hollow Athens
A day of fast running
Set three beautiful prizes on his hair,

40 And seven the Hellotian Games.
In Poseidon's sea-girt festivals
Too long would songs be to follow
Terpsias and Eritimos with their father Ptoiodoros.

For all your triumphs at Delphoi
And in the Lion's Grove I strive with many
In the multitude of your honours.
45 Truly I should not know
How to tell rightly
The number of stones in the sea.

III

– In everything the Mean is right, and to know
The Moment is best.
In the convoy of all I sail my own course.
50 I shall tell of the counsel of men long ago
And of war with surpassing heroes,
Nor lie about Korinth or Sisyphos
Most cunning in wits like a God,
And Medeia, who in her father's despite
Made a wedding for herself
And saved the ship Argo and her crew.

55 Of old also with valour
Before Dardanos' walls they were thought
To cut short the issue of battle on either side;
Some with the true breed of Atreus
Sought to win Helen back, the others
60 With might and main to hold them off.
When Glaukos came from Lykia, the Danaoi
Trembled at him. He boasted to them
That his father's dominion was in Peirana's city,
His deep estate and his hall.

He suffered much about the streams
In his longing to yoke the snaky Gorgon's child,
Pagasos, until Pallas brought to him
65 A gold-frontleted bridle. Straightway

His dream was the truth. She said:
'Do you sleep, King, son of Aiolos?
Come take this charm for the horse;
Sacrifice a glossy bull
And show it to the Father, the Tamer.'

IV

70 In the darkness the black-shielded Maiden
Seemed to say this to him in his sleep.
He leapt upright to his feet,
And seized the marvel that lay at his side.
In joy he found the seer of the land
75 And revealed to Koiranos' son
The whole end of the matter:
'On the Goddess's altar I slept
A whole night at your bidding;
And the daughter of Zeus herself,
Of him whose spear is the lightning,

Gave me the gold to break his spirit in.'
The prophet bade him: 'Obey the dream
80 Quickly, and when you have sacrificed
Strong-hooved beasts to the Earth-holder,
Straightway set up an altar
To Athana, goddess of horses.'
The gods' power makes it easy to win
What is beyond oath and beyond hope.
Truly strong Bellerophon strove and caught,
85 By stretching the gentle drug about its mouth,

The flying horse. He mounted it and therewith
Played the weapon-game in brazen armour;
And with it in time he slew
With shafts from the cold vales of the desolate air

The archer-host of Amazon women,
90 The fire-breathing Chimaira and the Solymoi.
On his doom I shall keep silence,
But the horse is kept on Olympos
In the stables of Zeus as of old.

V

– I must make a straight cast with my javelins
And not send the many shafts in my hand
95 Beside the mark. I have come
Of my own will to help
The Muses on shining thrones
And Oligaithos' sons. All they have done
At Isthmos and Nemea I shall make plain
In a short word; and a true statement on oath,
Heard sixty times at both places,
100 Shall be the sweet-tongued cry of a noble herald.

What they did at Olympia
Has, it seems, already been told;
What is to come, at the time I shall speak it clearly.
Now I have hope, but with God
105 Is the end. If the fate of the race goes on,
We shall leave this to Zeus
And to the Lord of the War-cry to do.
Six are their victories
Under the brow of Parnassos; and how many at Argos
  and Thebes,
And how many in Arkadian valleys,
The master-altar of the Lykaian God shall witness,

Pellana and Sikyon and Megara,
The well-walled precinct of the Aiakidai,
110 Eleusis and shining Marathon,

And the fine rich cities beneath Aitna's tall peak,
And Euboia, – if you search all Hellas,
You will find more than the eye can see.
   Up! with nimble feet I shall swim away.
Zeus Accomplisher, grant them modesty
115 And a fortune of sweet delights.

Olympian XIII was written in 464 B.C. and performed at Korinth, which Pindar visited for the occasion.

1 Xenophon had already won two victories at Olympia, and his father Thessalos one (34).

6–8 Lawfulness, Justice, and Peace are the qualities on which aristocratic communities like Korinth prided themselves.

10 'Pride . . . mother of surfeit'. Solon and Theognis make Surfeit the mother of Pride.

18–22 Korinth is credited with the invention of the dithyramb, the bit for horses, and the eagles on the crests of temples.

29–46 Enumeration of victories won by Xenophon and his kinsmen.

49 Pindar will go his own way in singing of familiar Korinthian themes.

52 Sisyphos, king of Korinth, got back from death by a trick.

53 Medeia marries Jason against the will of her father Aietas.

55 In the Trojan War Korinthians fought on the Achaian side under Euchenor, on the Trojan side under Glaukos.

63–92 Myth of Bellerophon and the winged horse, Pagasos. The latter was the national emblem of Korinth, displayed on its coins.

63 Pagasos was the child of the Gorgon.

69 The 'Tamer' is a cult-name for Poseidon.

75 The seer Polyeidos was son of Koiranos.

86 ff. The feats of Bellerophon on Pagasos.

91–2 Bellerophon tries to scale the sky on Pagasos, and is thrown. Pindar may suggest a warning against pride in mentioning this.

97 The Oligaithidai are the victor's family.

106–13 More victories.

NEMEAN X

For Theaios of Argos, a wrestler

I

The city of Danaos
And his fifty daughters on shining thrones,
Sing of it, Graces,
Of Argos, home of Hera, fit for the Gods.
It is aflame with glories past number
Because of bold doings.
Long are the tales of what Perseus did to the Gorgon
    Medoisa,
5   And many the cities of Egypt founded by Epaphos' hands;
Nor went Hypermestra astray
When she kept in its sheath
Her single, dissentient sword.

Once the fair Bright-eyed One
Made Diomedes a god undying,
And at Thebes the earth,
Thunderstruck with the bolts of Zeus,
Swallowed Oikleës' son, the battle's cloud.
10 In lovely-haired women it is first from of old;
Zeus proved the truth of this
When he came to Alkmana and to Danaä.
In Adrastos' father and in Lynkeus he grafted
The heart's fruit on upstanding right.

He nursed the spear of Amphitryon,
Who was foremost in fortune and came to kinship with
    him,

15 When in armour of bronze he spoiled the Teleboai.
In his likeness the King of Immortals came into his
          palace
And brought the unconquerable seed of Herakles,
Whose bride Youth walks on Olympus
At the side of the Mother, the Match-maker,
Most beautiful of goddesses.

II

My breath is too short to rehearse all the fine things
20 That belong to the precinct of Argos;
The boredom of men is heavy to counter.
Nevertheless, awake the fine strings of the harp
And turn your thoughts to wrestling.
The brazen struggle hurries the people
To the sacrifice of oxen to Hera
And the verdict of the Games,
Where Theaios, son of Oulias, conquered twice,
And found forgetfulness of toils he had lightly borne.

25 Once he routed the host of Hellas at Pytho,
And fortunate was his coming
To the crown at the Isthmos and Nemea.
He gave ploughland to the Muses
When he won three times in the gates of the sea,
Three times by Adrastos' rules on holy ground.
Father Zeus, on his heart's desire his lips are silent;
Every end of doing rests with thee –
30 But not with a sluggard's heart
Does he ask for favour wrongly,
But brings endurance with him.

I sing what is known to him
And to all who strive for the peaks of the highest Games.

The foremost, which Herakles founded, belongs to Pisa,
Yet in prelude sweet Athenian voices
Have twice extolled him in their festivals;
35   And in fire-baked clay the olive's fruit
Has come to Hera's people of noble men
In the pots' richly patterned walls.

III

Over the far-famed race
Of your mother's clan, Theaios,
Watches renown for success in the Games,
With the Graces often to help and Tyndareos' sons.
40   If I were kin of Thrasyklos and Antias,
I should hold it right
Not to veil the light of my eyes from Argos.
For with how many victories
Has this horse-breeding city of Proitos burst into flower
In the Gulf of Korinth,
And four times over the men of Kleonai.

From Sikyon they came silvered with wine-cups,
From Pellana with clothes of soft wool on their backs.
45   But I cannot add up the multitudinous bronze,
– It takes too long to count –
Which Kleitor and Tegea,
The Achaians' high-set towns and the Lykaian Hill,
Set in the race-track of Zeus
To be won by strong feet and hands.

Since Kastor and his brother Polydeukes
50   Came to be guests of Pamphaes,
It is no wonder that this race begets good athletes.
For they who watch over Sparta's broad places,
With Hermes and Herakles,
Make the rule of the Games to prosper,

And care for good men exceedingly. Truly
The breed of the Gods may be trusted.

IV

55 Turn and turn about they pass
One day with their loving father Zeus,
The other hidden by earth in Therapna's caverns,
And fulfil a like fate.
This life, and not to be fully a god and live in the sky,
Polydeukes chose, when Kastor was killed in war.
60 For Idas, in anger over some oxen,
Struck him with a spear's bronze point.

Lynkeus looked out from Taygetos
And saw them sitting in an oak's dry trunk;
For his eye was the sharpest of all on earth.
With racing feet they came at once and quickly
Devised a great enterprise,
And Zeus worked terrible suffering for them,
65 The sons of Aphareus.
For straightway in chase came Leda's son,
And they stood on defence by their father's tomb.

From it they ripped Death's ornament,
A polished stone,
And flung it on Polydeukes' breast.
But they did not break him or drive him back.
With his quick spear he jumped upon them
70 And drove the bronze into Lynkeus' lungs;
And on Idas Zeus threw a fiery smoking thunderbolt.

V

To his strong brother quickly came back Tyndareos' son
And found him not yet dead

But shaking with gasps in his breath.
75 He let hot tears fall and lifted his voice in lament:
'Father Kronion, what release shall there be from sorrows?
Give death to me also, Master, with him.
Honour goes from one who has lost his friends,
And in trouble few among men may be trusted

To share in suffering.' He spoke,
And Zeus came before him
80 And spoke this word clearly:
'You are my son,
But this man was begotten of mortal seed
By his hero father,
Who drew after me to your mother.
Yet now I give you this choice:
If you would escape from death and from hated old age
And dwell on Olympus with me
And with Athana and with black-speared Ares,

85 This lot may be yours.
But if you fight for your brother,,
And are minded to share with him in all things alike,
You may live half beneath the earth,
And half in the sky's golden palaces.'
He spoke, and Polydeukes set
No double counsel in his heart,
90 But freed the eye, and then the voice
Of bronze-belted Kastor.

Nemean X seems to have been written about 464 B.C. for an Argive who won not at Nemea but in local games at the festival of Hera.

1–18 The first triad deals with the glories of Argos.

1 Danaos was the father of fifty daughters, of whom all but one was forced to marry an Egyptian suitor.

4 Perseus was born in Argos.

5 Epaphos, the son of Io, founded Memphis and other Egyptian cities.

6 Hypermestra was the only daughter of Danaos who did not kill her suitor but married him.

7 Athana made Diomedes a god in the Adriatic.

8–9 Amphiaraos, son of Oikleës, was swallowed up in the earth in the war of the Seven against Thebes.

11 Alkmana, wife of Amphitryon, bears Herakles to Zeus.

12 Talaos is father of Adrastos, Lynkeus the son of Aphareus, both renowned for their wisdom.

15 Zeus begets Herakles by assuming the likeness of Amphitryon who is away fighting the Teleboai.

19–36 The second triad tells of the victories won by Theaios.

24 Oulias is father of Theaios.

28 The Adrastos games were at Argos.

35–6 The prizes at Athens were painted pots.

37–54 The third triad tells of victories won by the family of Theaios.

49–54 A connexion is made between the present victor and the Dioskouroi. In the past Pamphaes used to entertain them. With Hermes and Herakles they look after games.

55–90 The last two triads tell the story of the last fight of the Dioskouroi against the sons of Aphareus, Idas and Lynkeus.

60 Pindar hurries past the real reason for the quarrel, which included women as well as oxen.

62 Lynkeus sees the Dioskouroi from a great distance.

72 Tyndareos' son is Polydeukes, who comes to the help of Kastor.

90 Polydeukes' decision brings his brother back to life.

PYTHIAN V

For Arkesilas of Kyrene, winner in the chariot-race

I

The strength of wealth is wide,
When a mortal man
Has it from Fortune's hands, and mixes with it
An unstained nobleness: and, whom it follows,
Many are his friends.
5   You, Arkesilas, for whom the Gods care,
Have won it from the high steps of your glorious life
Through Kastor, gold-charioted lord.
After the storm-shower
10 He smiles fair weather down on your happy hearth.

The wise wear with a fairer grace
This power which Gods have given.
You who walk in righteousness
Have great prosperity around you.
15 First, you are king of mighty cities
(Your royal eye
Looks on no title so honourable
As this, engrafted on your heart)
20 And today too you are happy, your horses
Have won your prayer
At the feast of glorious Pytho,
And you have received this visit, a triumph of men,

The light of Apollo's eyes. –
Forget not, while you are sung of
In Aphrodita's sweet garden at Kyrene,
25 To set a God as the cause

Over all things and to love
Karrhotos the best of your companions.
He did not come bringing
Excuse, the daughter of late-wise Afterthought,
To the halls where Battos' sons
Of right bear rule –
30 No, but he proved your chariot the best
While a guest by the water of Kastalia,
And set the prize on your hair,

II

His reins untangled, where swift feet go
Twelve times around the holy field.
He broke nothing of his strong-harnessed car:
It is hung on high,
35 All that cunning handwork that he took with him
Past the Krisean Hill
Into the level field, the glade of the God.
The Cypress Chamber keeps it
40 Hard by that image
Which the Kretan bowmen set
In a shrine on Parnassos – a tree-trunk uprooted whole.

With glad heart then you may meet him
Who has done you so fine service.
45 – On you, son of Alexibios,
Is the light of the lovely-haired Graces:
Happy, for if your labour was great,
In noblest words is your memorial.
Among forty drivers who fell
50 You brought your chariot
Whole, with unflinching heart;
And now from the splendid encounter you have come
To Libya's plain and the city of your fathers.

There is no man, nor shall be,
Without his portion of troubles.
55 Yet, after one thing and another,
Still the old happiness of Battos clings,
A tower of the city,
A most bright eye to strangers.
From him in terror
Loud-roaring lions fled
When he unloosed on them his seafarer's tongue.
60 Apollo, the leader of the way,
Delivered the wild beasts to terrible fear,
That his vice-regent in Kyrene
Should know his oracles come true.

III

He grants to men and women
Healing from grievous sicknesses:
65 His is the harp. He gives to whom he will
The Muse, and brings into the heart
Law, that thinks not of battle:
In the Cave of Prophecy he is to be found.
Thence he established in Lakedaimon,
70 In Argos and holy Pylos, the valiant children
Of Herakles and Aigimios.
And he proclaims
My well-prized glory that I have from Sparta.

For thence were sprung
The men who came to Thera, the Aigeidai,
75 Kinsmen to me,
(Not without Gods, a destiny led them):
From them
The Feast of Friends, and the sacrifices, came
To us, who at your banquet,

80 Apollo Karneios,
Honour the strong-built city of Kyrene,
The city of the bronze-armoured strangers,
Antenor's sons from Troy.
They came with Helen, after they saw
Their country in smoke

85 From the God of war.
    That was a race of horsemen;
And others, who found them,
Were gentle, offering sacrifices and gifts,
Aristoteles' men,
Whom he carried in swift ships, cleaving
A deep path in the sea.
He enlarged the groves of the Gods, and made
90 For Apollo's processions, which keep his people safe,
A straight hewn way,
Level and paved,
Sounding with the tramp of horses.
And there at the far end of the Market Place
He lies apart in death.

IV

He dwelt in bliss among men: and afterwards, a hero,
95 The people worshipped him.
Apart, before the Palace,
Are others who have found death,
Holy Kings: their mighty greatness
Is drenched with delicate dew
100 When the revellers pour libation: and deep
In the earth, their heart listens.
This is their bliss: in this delight their son
Arkesilas shares in his right.
His name in the young men's song

Let Phoibos of the Gold Sword cry aloud.

105 Now that from Pytho comes
The sweet of triumph, the ransoming of cost.
This music of delight!
Lo, there is a man whom the wise praise.
I will say what is said:
110 He pastures a mind and a tongue beyond his youth:
With the long wings of his courage
He is an eagle among the birds:
He is the strength of victory like a wall.
The Muses know him
Winged from his mother's lap.
115 He is proved a right charioteer:

He has entered the lists of the noble arts of this land
Boldly. Now God is kind to him
And establishes his power.
And in years to come, you blessed sons of Kronos,
In his acts and his counsels
120 Grant him the like. Let no stormy wind
Of autumn overwhelm his days.
The great mind of Zeus
Is pilot of the doom of men whom he loves.
I pray Him at Olympia
To add His glory to the House of Battos.

In 462 B.C. Arkesilas IV, king of Kyrene, sent a chariot-team to the Pythian Games, which its driver, Karrhotos, brought to victory. *Pythian V* was sung at Kyrene probably in the following year. It is not likely that Pindar himself was present.

24 Kyrene is called the garden of Aphrodita because of its fertility.

26 Karrhotos, the charioteer, was a personal friend of Pindar.

39–42 The reins and gear of the chariot are dedicated in a wooden chamber close to a wooden Cretan statue made of a single block and presumably of some antiquity.

45 The son of Alexibios is Karrhotos.

57 Battos, the founder of the royal family at Kyrene, asked the Delphic Oracle how to heal his stammer, and was told to found Kyrene. The lions fled from his stammer in terror.

63 Kyrene was famous for its doctors, which were said to be the best after those of Kroton.

69–73 Through the Aigid clan to which he belongs, Pindar claims kinship with Sparta, Argos, Pylos, and Thera, where the clan has representatives.

80 The Dorian feast of the Karneia is now being celebrated at Kyrene.

82 The earliest colonists of Kyrene were said to be Trojans after the sack of Troy.

87 Aristotelès is another name for the first Battos.

90–93 The song is sung on the paved street of Battos, at the end of which is his tomb.

96 The dead kings hear the song from their tombs.

107–16 Praise of Arkesilas.

121 Read χρόνον.

124 Pindar prays that Arkesilas may win an Olympian victory.

PYTHIAN IV

For Arkesilas of Kyrene, winner in the chariot-race

I

Today, Muse, you must stand by the side of a friend,
By the King of Kyrene, the land of good horses:
And when Arkesilas holds his triumph
Swell the gale of your songs,
Paying your debt to Lato's Twins, and to Pytho,
5   Where once, when Apollo was in his land,
The priestess – she who sits by the gold eagles of Zeus –
Ordained Battos a leader of men
Into fruitful Libya.
He must straightway leave his holy island
And build a city
Of charioteers
On a silver breast of the earth.

To bring back the word of Medeia
10   In the seventeenth generation,
Which at Thera once Aietas' terrible child
Breathed from immortal lips, the Kolchians' Queen –
And thus she spoke:
To the seed of Gods, to the sailors of Jason the fighter:
'Hear, sons of high-hearted men and of Gods!
I tell you, from this wave-beaten land shall go
A stock, and shall beteem the daughter of Epaphos,
And cities shall rise
15   And the world know it
In the place where Zeus Ammon stands.

Instead of the short-finned dolphins

They shall have swift horses, and reins for oars:
They shall drive the stormfoot chariots.
The Omen, that shall make
20   Thera mother-city of mighty cities,
Was given, where Lake Tritonis flows to the sea,
To Euphamos once
(A guest-gift from the God in a man's likeness)
A Clod. Euphamos, alighting from the bows,
Took it, and Father Zeus, the son of Kronos,
Well pleased rang out in thunder.

II

He found us slinging the bronze-jawed anchor
25   Beside the prow, swift Argo's bridle.
I had bidden them haul her, our sea-timber, ashore,
And he had borne her from Ocean
Twelve days across earth's lonely ridges.
Out of his solitudes then
The God appeared
Clothed in the bright shape of a reverend lord:
30   And friendly words he began,
As a good host when strangers come,
Begins with his offers of supper.

But we spoke of our sweet road home
And could not stay. He told us his name
Eurypylos, son of the undying
Shaker and Holder of Earth.
And he knew our hurry: and there and then
35   Took a clod in his right hand, fain to offer
What gift he could;
And the hero did not refuse it.
He leaped to the beach, and clasping hand in hand
Took the piece of earth divine, –

But a wave broke,
I hear, and washed it
Overboard into the sea

40 At evening, and it went with the waters of the deep.
O often I bade the servants we had for our ease
Keep it safe: but their souls forgot.
So now against this isle has been washed
The undying seed of Libya's wide meadows,
Out of due time.
For had he come home, and cast it
Beside Hell's mouth in the earth,
Had he come to holy Tainaros, – he
Euphamos, son of Poseidon the captain of horse,
45 Born on Kaphisos' banks of Europa, Tityos' child, –

III

Then the blood of his grandsons' grandsons after him,
With a Danaan host, had taken that wide mainland.
For then, behold!
Men coming from great Lakedaimon,
From the gulf of Argos and from Mykenai!
50 – But now, he shall lie with foreign women
And get a chosen race: who shall come to this island
(For the Gods will care for them)
And have a son to be lord
Of those dark-clouded plains.
Him one day
In that gold-stored House
Phoibos shall tell in oracles

55 (When in later days he comes down to the Pythian
shrine)
To carry cities in ships
To the land where Neilos dwells, the son of Kronos.'

Medeia's words filed past: and the godlike heroes
Kept silent and still, and bowed their heads,
Listening to her deep wisdom.
   O happy son of Polymnastos!
To you, as was here foretold,
The oracle of the Delphic Bee gave glory
60 In her unprompted cry,
Bidding you three times 'Hail!'
Foreshown
Kyrene's King to be.

(You were asking
About your stammering tongue, might the Gods
    release you.)
And later in time, even today,
There flowers, as when spring puts out her reddest
    blossoms,
65 The eighth generation, Arkesilas.
He has got from Apollo, and from Pytho
A name for chariot-driving
Among the peoples around.
I will offer to the Muses
Him, and the Ram's Fleece of Gold.
For the Minyai sailed to find it; and from that root
Sprang up the honours of the house
About whose goings is God.

IV

70 What was the beginning of their voyage?
And what danger held them in strong adamantine bolts?
– It was appointed that Pelias
Must die by the hands of Aiolos' proud sons
Or their unrelenting counsels.
A prophecy came to him, chilling his wary heart,

Spoken at the midmost navel-stone
Of earth, fair-forested mother:
75 'Let him beware at all costs
The man with one sandal,
When he comes from the steadings in the hills
To the sunny plains of great Iolkos,

Stranger be he or townsman.' In time he came,
With two spears, a terrible man.
And he wore two kinds of clothing:
80 The garment of the Magnesian land
Fitted close on his marvellous limbs,
And a leopard-skin over it
Kept off the shivering rains.
His bright locks of hair, not cut and cast away,
Flamed all down his back.
And at once, when he came,
He stood testing his never-flinching heart
85 Where the people thronged in the main square.

None knew him: yet despite their amazement
Thus spoke one:
'This is not Apollo, I think,
No, nor Aphrodita's bronze-charioted lord,
And they say that in bright Naxos
The sons of Iphimedeia died,
Otos, and you, daring lord Ephialtas:
90 And the swift arrow of Artemis
Caught Tityos, sped from that unconquered quiver,
That a man be fain to choose
Attainable loves '

V

So they spoke
One to another in question and answer.

But then drove up, with his mules and burnished car,
95 Pelias, in headlong haste.
Amazed at once he stared and knew well
The single sandal on the right foot.
But he hid his fear in his heart, and said:
'What sort of country do you say is yours, O
    stranger?
And pray, what gutter-bred wench
Dropped you from her aged womb?
100 No loathsome, filthy lies, but tell me your race.'

And the other answered without fear and gently:
'Cheiron I name my master
And men shall see it. I come from the cave,
From Chariklo and Philyra,
The Centaur's holy daughters who nursed me.
I have brought twenty years to an end, and in them
105 Have done, nor said, nothing to shame me.
And I have come home
Claiming the ancient honour of my father
(Now against right overruled)
Which Zeus once gave
To Aiolos and his sons.

I am told that Pelias the transgressor
Gave way to his pale heart
110 And stole this by force
From my parents, who ruled of right.
When the sun first opened my eyes, they feared
That violent prince's malice:
So they darkened the house and made a keening
As if I had died,
And amongst the wailing of women
Stealthily they sent me away
In swaddling bands of purple,

115 And Night knew the secret of our road.
So they gave me to Cheiron, Kronos' son, for nurture.

VI

You have heard the sum of my story.
But where
Is the house of my fathers that rode white horses?
Good citizens, tell me clearly.
I am Aison's son, a man of the land,
Nor am I come to a strange country
Belonging to others.
By my name Jason the godlike Beast addressed me.'
120 He spoke; and when he went in, his father's eyes
Knew him, and tears welled down
From his old eyelids:
For in his soul
He was glad, seeing
His chosen son, the fairest of men.

And his two brothers came to that house
125 At the fame of the man. From near
Pheras came, leaving the fountain Hypereia,
From Messana Amythaon.
And soon Admatos came and Melampos,
For their hearts yearned to their cousin.
– With due feasting, and words honey-sweet,
Jason their host made pleasant entertainment
130 And long stretched-out delight, five nights
Without ceasing
And five days
Gathering the great luxurious hours.

But on the sixth day, with sober words
He let his kinsman know all from the beginning:
And they gave him heed,

And he leaped up quickly from his couch, and they with
    him,
And went to Pelias' hall
135 And made haste and stood within.
When the King heard them, himself came forth to them,
The son of Tyro, lovely-haired queen;
And Jason with soft voice, let smooth words fall,
Laying a foundation of wise speech:
'Son of Poseidon of the Rock,

VII

The hearts of men are perhaps too quick
140 At choosing a smart advantage rather than right
(Though the next day the taste is wry in the mouth).
But I and you must rule our wrath
And weave our future fortune.
You know as well as I, one womb
Bore Kretheus and Salmoneus hardy in cunning,
From whom in the third generation ourselves sprang,
Who look on the golden strength of the sun.
145 – The Fates recoil
When men of one blood
Hating each other, lose sight of shame.

We must not take, you and I,
Swords of biting bronze or javelins
To divide our father's honours.
The sheep and the tawny herds of oxen
I yield you, and all the fields,
150 Which you stole from my parents and live on,
Fattening your substance.
Nourish with these your house, it irks me little.
But there is the sceptre of absolute rule,
And the throne on which the son of Kretheus sat

And gave straight judgements
To a people of horsemen.
To spare both of us sorrow

155 Let me have these;
And no fresh evil come of them!'
– So he spoke: and gently too
Pelias answered him:
'I will do as you say.
But already the sere end of life attends me
And your youth bursts into flower.
You have power to lay the wrath of those in earth.
160 Phrixos is calling, that someone redeem his ghost,
And, going to the halls of Aietas, fetch
The thick-piled Fleece
Of the Ram, by whom he was saved of old
From the sea,

VIII

And from the godless knives of his step-mother.
A marvellous dream came and told me of this.
I have asked the oracle of Kastalia:
"Shall I follow this up?", and he bids me find
At once the crew for a ship.
165 – Achieve this task, so please you; and I swear
I will let you be sole ruler and king.
Let Him be our strong oath,
Zeus the Witness, the father of both our races.'
So they approved
This covenant:
And these two parted, but as for Jason, already

170 He was sending messengers everywhere
That a quest was afoot.
– And soon there came, that never tired of battle,

The sons of Zeus Kronidas,
Of Alkmana of the dancing eyelids and of Leda:
And two tall-crested men, the Earth-Shaker's seed,
In the proudness of valour,
From Pylos and Cape Tainaros:
– Fair was the fame they won,
175 Euphamos, and you, strong Periklymenos.
From Apollo's house
The lute-player came,
The father of songs, ever-worshipped Orpheus.

Hermes of the golden wand
Sent his twin sons to that long stretch of labour,
Echion one (O loud exultation of youth),
The other Erytos. Quick came two
180 Who dwelt round the roots of Pangaion:
For gladly with laughing heart and swiftly
Their father Boreas, King of Winds,
Sent Zetes and Kalaïs – men,
Yet scarlet feathers ruffled upon their backs.
And in these sons of Gods Hera kindled
That all-persuading sweet desire

IX

185 For the ship Argo, that none be left behind
To nurse at his mother's side a ventureless life,
But, even though he die,
Find in his own valour the fairest enchantment
With others young as he.
   They came to the port of Iolkos, the finest of sailors,
And Jason marshalled all, and approved them.
190 And the seer Mopsos, that watched the Gods' will for him
In birds and holy sortilege,
Bade with good heart

The host be started.
They hung the anchor over the prow; and then

The Captain at the stern
Held in his hands a gold cup, and called
On the Father of the Sons of Heaven,
Zeus, whose spear is the lightning,
195 On the swift rushing of the waves, the winds,
On the nights and the paths of the sea;
For days of kind weather, and the sweet road home at
    last.
From the clouds answered back to him
The assenting voice of thunder,
And the lightnings flashed and tore the sky.
The heroes found fresh breath of courage,
For they believed
The omens of God.
200 The Seer of Signs called to them

To fall to the oars,
And he put sweet hopes into them: under their rapid
    hands
The oars insatiably fell and rose.
A south wind blew, and before it
They reached the Unwelcoming Sea.
They marked a holy acre there
For Poseidon of the Deep
205 And there was a red herd of Thracian bulls
And a hollow altar newly fashioned of stone.
    They were running toward deep danger
And prayed to the Lord of Ships

X

To escape the awful onset
Of the Clashing Rocks. Two they were, and alive,

And they rolled swifter
210 Than the howling winds charge past.
But that sailing of the sons of Gods
Brought them to an end.
   After that they came to the River Phasis
And matched their might
Among the dark-faced Kolchians,
In the very presence of Aietas.
But from Olympos the Queen of sharpest arrows
Bound past loosing
The dappled wryneck
215 To the four spokes of a wheel:

She, the Kypros-born, for the first time brought
The maddening bird to men.
She taught Aison's wise son
What sorceries he must chant, and Medeia forget
To honour those who begot her,
And her heart be all on fire for lovely Hellas
And tremble under the lash of love.
220 She showed him at once
How to achieve his father's tasks:
With olive-oil she made an enchantment against hard
    pains
And gave it to him for anointing.
And they swore to make a sweet marriage one with
    another.

But when Aietas
Dragged forth the adamantine plough in the midst of
    them
225 And the oxen who breathed from yellow nostrils
A flame of burning fire,
And hoof after bronze-shod hoof ripped up the ground –
He took them and forced them to the yoke

Alone, and straight was the furrow he ploughed as he
    drove them:
He cast up the clods, and clove earth's back
230 A fathom deep; and thus he spoke:
'Let the King do this, the captain of the ship!
Let him do this, I say,
And have for his own the immortal coverlet,

XI

The Fleece, glowing with matted skeins of gold.'
He spoke; and Jason
Threw off his saffron clothing, and trusting in God
Assayed the task.
And the fire did not make him flinch,
Through the strange woman's words, that strong
    enchantress.
He, grasping the plough,
235 Harnessed perforce the oxen's necks, and driving
In those huge flanks a steady goad
With violence he achieved the appointed distance.
And, speechless through
His grief, Aietas
Howled in amazement at his might.

To the mighty man his comrades
240 Stretched out their hands, and gathered grass to crown
    him:
With sweet words they caressed him.
Then the Sun's wondrous child
Told him where the shining Skin
Had been stretched by Phrixos' sword (and there
Was a labour where, he hoped, he yet may fail).
It lay in a snake's den,
Caught on the monster's raging teeth

245 That was thicker and longer
Than a ship
Of fifty oars
Made by the smiting iron.

The journey is long on the high road:
Time presses me, and I know a short path,
(In the wisdom of song I am the leader of many).
– He slew by cunning
The snake with glaring eyes and bright-scaled back;
250 O Arkesilas,
He stole Medeia, she willing, – she, who was Pelias'
death.
They came to the depths of Ocean, to the Red Sea,
To the Land of Lemnians,
Women the slayers of men.
There in bodily games they proved their might
(A garment for the prize)

XII

And there they wedded. Then it was, in foreign furrows
255 A day, or a night,
Received the destined seed
Of your house's sunlike fortune.
For then the race of Euphamos took root,
Growing thereafter always higher.
They mixed first in Lakedaimon's dwellings,
They went to live in the island
Once called Loveliest.
And after that Lato's son
Gave you Libya's plain, for the Gods love you,
260 To enrich and govern
The holy city
Of Kyrene on her throne of gold

Since judgement and right counsel are yours.
  Try now the Art of Oidipous.
If a man with a keen axe-blade
Lops the branches of a great oak,
Defiling the beauty that men gazed at –
265 Though its fruit has perished, yet it gives
Witness of itself, when it comes at last
In winter to the fire,
Or rests on the upright pillars of a master,
Doing sad labour in a stranger's house
While its own land is desolate.

270 – But you can heal in the very nick of time.
You give light, and Paian adds honour to it.
Stretch out a gentle hand, to tend
A sore wound.
It is easy even for weaker men than you
To shake a city, but hard indeed
To set it back in the land,
Unless a God be suddenly there, the pilot of kings.
275 For you
The web of these bright years is being woven.
Have patience for the sake of Kyrene's happiness
To give it all your care.

XIII

Remember a saying of Homer's, and cherish it –
'A good messenger,' he said, 'heightens
The honour of any errand.'
Even the Muse's stature
Is more, if she be well reported.
There was known in Kyrene
280 And to that most famous hall of Battos
A man of just heart, Damophilos,

Young in the eyes of boys, but in counsel
An old man with a hundred garner'd years,
He robs of loudness
The slanderous tongue.
He has learned to hate the insolent,

285   He does not strive counter to the good,
None of his purposes tarry; for very swift
Is the Moment for a man.
He has seen it: Time is his servant now, and not running
    away.
– They say there is nothing more sorrowful
Than to see joy and stand perforce outside.
290   Atlas indeed still wrestles with the sky
Far from his father's country and his possessions:
Yet deathless Zeus
Set free the Titans.
In time the wind sags, and we hoist

New sails. – But now, he cries,
He has done with foul illness at last, and he sees home.
Near Apollo's fountain
295   He shall lie at the feast, and yield his heart to youth
Often, and playing his painted harp,
Where men know music, shall touch the hands of peace:
Giving sorrow to none, and having
No wrong from his fellow-townsmen.
And perhaps he will tell, Arkesilas,
What a well of immortal words he found
When lately a guest at Thebes.

Pythian IV celebrates the same victory as *Pythian V* but seems to have
been sung at the court of Arkesilas. It is by far the longest of Pindar's
surviving poems and owes something to the epic despite its formal
lyrical art.

1–8 The poem begins with recalling the occasion on which the first Battos was told by the Delphic Oracle to found a city in Africa.

9–69 The Prelude. Through a prophecy once spoken by Medeia Pindar explains why North Africa was not colonized much earlier by Greeks. Her prophecy was fulfilled much later when men from Thera, where the prophecy was given and where Battos was born, went to Africa.

14 The 'daughter of Epaphos' is Libya.

16 Zeus Ammon had an oracular temple in an oasis in the desert.

19 The omen is about to be mentioned – the clod offered to Euphamos. It is a sign that the Argonauts will rule Africa, but when it is washed away at sea (38 ff.) the prophecy is delayed. The promise comes from Eurypylos, son of Poseidon.

43 ff. If Euphamos had placed the clod in the holy cave at Tainaron, Greeks would have colonized Africa in four generations from then.

50 ff. As it is, events have had to wait for Battos to be sent by Apollo.

64 The preliminaries being finished, Pindar prepares the way for his myth – the quest of the Golden Fleece. It is told as a story for its own sake and because Arkesilas is descended from an Argonaut.

70–254 The tale of the quest.

89 Otos and Ephialtas, sons of Poseidon, renowned for their size and beauty.

119 'the godlike Beast' is Cheiron.

120 Jason's father is Aison.

135 The son of Tyro is Pelias.

152 The son of Kretheus is Aison.

159–62 Phrixos was saved by the ram with a golden fleece from being drowned at sea, as his step-mother, who was in love with him, wished. The ram's fleece was in Kolchis, strongly guarded.

208–10 The Argonauts pass safely through the Symplegades or Clashing Rocks.

214 Aphrodita uses the wryneck to work a magical spell on Medeia and make her fall in love with Jason.

247 The myth really ends with the recovery of the Fleece, but Pindar touches lightly on some later events.

250 Medeia killed Pelias by claiming to rejuvenate him by magic.

258 The island called Loveliest is Thera.

262 Pindar changes his direction and sets a riddle. It concerns a kinsman of the king, one Damophilos, who recently conspired against Arkesilas and is now in exile in Greece. There Pindar met him, and he now pleads for clemency to him. The riddle of the oak means that Damophilos can be either wasted or turned to a profitable use.

270 Now is the time to heal the wound.

277 The actual words of Homer come from *Iliad XIV*, 207, 'this too is a good thing, when a messenger says what is fitting'.

290 If Zeus relented about the Titans, Arkesilas can about Damophilos.

We do not know what happened, but Pindar's hopes were not fulfilled, since soon afterwards Arkesilas was killed by his own people.

NEMEAN VI

For Alkimidas of Aigina, winner in the boys' wrestling

I

Single is the race, single
Of men and of gods;
From a single mother we both draw breath.
But a difference of power in everything
Keeps us apart;
For the one is as Nothing, but the brazen sky
Stays a fixed habitation for ever.
5 Yet we can in greatness of mind
Or of body be like the Immortals,
Tho' we know not to what goal
By day or in the nights
Fate has written that we shall run.

Even now Alkimidas gives visible witness
That his race is like the fruitful fields
Which change about
10 And now give men abounding life from the soil,
Now rest again and pick up strength.
He has come from Nemea's well-loved Games,
A boy in the struggle,
Who follows this calling from Zeus;
He has been revealed a hunter
And had good sport in the wrestling.

15 He plants his feet in the kindred tracks
Of his father's father, Praxidamas;
For he, an Olympian victor,
First brought twigs from Alpheos to the Aiakidai;

He was crowned five times at the Isthmus,
20 Thrice at Nemea,
And saved Sokleidas from oblivion,
Who was first of Hagesidamos' sons.

II

To his delight three prize-winners
Reached the peak of prowess by tasting of toil.
With good fortune from God
25 Boxing has proved no other house
To hold more crowns in the heart of all Hellas.
I hope with this big word
To hit the mark as with a shot from the bow.
    Come, Muse, waft straight to him
The glorious gale of your words;
For when men pass away,

30 Songs and tables bring back
Their noble achievements for them.
Of these the Bassidai have no lack.
A clan renowned of old,
They convoyed their own hymns of praise
And could give the Pierians' ploughmen
Many a song of their lordly doings.
In rich Pytho one from the blood of this land,
35 His hands bound in the boxing-strap,
Kallias, won, the favourite

Of gold-haired Lato's children;
And at Kastalia in the evening
The Graces' loud song shed flame on him.
The bridges of the unwearying sea
In the Feast of the Dwellers Around
40 And the slaughter of bulls in the second year

Honoured Kreontidas in Poseidon's acre,
And the Lion's grass crowned him in victory
Under the shaggy ancient hills of Phleious.

III

45 For tellers of tales
Wide avenues open on every side
To grace this glorious island.
For the Aiakidai gave them
A surpassing destiny
And revealed their great acts of prowess.
Their fame flies far over the earth and across the sea.
It leaped even to the Ethiopians
50 When Memnon came not home.
Heavy for them was the fight into which Achilles fell
When he came down from his chariot to the ground

And slew the son of the shining Dawn
With the edge of his furious sword.
This theme men of old found a road for traffic;
I too follow and make it my care.
55 But the wave that rolls at times at the ship's keel
Is said most to trouble every man's heart.
On my willing back I shoulder a double burden
And have come to tell the news
Of this twenty-fifth prayer answered

From the Games which men call holy.
60 Alkimidas, you have added it
To your illustrious race.
Twice the flowers of the Olympian Festival
By the precinct of Kronos
Were stolen from you in your boyhood
By the wanton fall of a lot.

To a dolphin in the sea
65 I would match Melesias for quickness,
Charioteer of hands and strength.

Nemean VI was possibly composed about 461 B.C.

1–7 Gods and men are both born from a single mother, Earth, but differ immeasurably in the degree of their power and security.

16 ff. The descent of the family is Hagesimachos – Sokleidas – Praxidamas – Theon – Alkimidas.

33 'the Pierians' ploughmen' are poets.

39 'the bridges of the . . . sea' are the Isthmus of Corinth.

64 It is not clear how the lot worked, but it is possible that it settled the order of contests, and thus anyone who drew an early place had an advantage in that he could recover before the next round.

65 Melesias is the Athenian trainer.

OLYMPIAN VIII

For Alkimedon of Aigina, winner in the boys' wrestling

I

Mother of the gold-crowned Games,
Olympia, mistress of truth,
Where seers interpret burnt offerings
And test the bright thunderer Zeus
If he has any word about men
5   Who yearn in their hearts to win great glory
And a breathing space after toil.

In return for reverence
Men's prayers are accomplished.
   O wooded place of Pisa by Alpheos,
10   Welcome this company and wearing of garlands.
His glory is great for ever
Whom your glittering prize attends.
To each man come different goods, and many
Are the paths of success
When the Gods give help.

15   Timosthenes, fate has allotted
Your race to Zeus for its own God.
He made you renowned at Nemea,
And Alkimedon by Kronos' Hill
An Olympian conqueror.
He was lovely to see, and his acts
Did not dishonour his beauty,
20   When he won in the wrestling and proclaimed
His fatherland, long-oared Aigina.

There Saviour Right is honoured
At the side of Zeus, the strangers' God

II

Most among men.
            When the balance
Is heavy and heavily sways,
25 It is hard to judge
With clear head at the right moment.
An ordinance of the Immortals
Placed this sea-girt land
As a holy pillar for strangers from everywhere,
– May Time rising ahead
Not weary of doing this –

30 A Dorian people watch over it
From Aiakos' time.
   Him Lato's Son and Poseidon, who rules afar,
When they started to make a crown for Ilion,
Called to share the work at the wall;
For it was fated
That, when wars were awakened
35 In fights and destruction of cities,
It should breathe up angry smoke.

Three yellow snakes, when the town was just built,
Jumped on the wall. Two fell down
And straightway in amazement threw up their lives,
40 But one leapt with a cry.
Apollo pondered the adverse sign
And forthwith cried: 'By the work of your hands, hero,
Pergamos shall be taken,
– So says a vision sent to me
From Kronos' son, loud-thundering Zeus –

III

45 Not without your sons. It shall be broken
In the first and the third generations.'
So spoke the God truly, and drove in haste
To Xanthos, and the Amazons, the fine horse-women,
And to Ister.
And the Trident-lifter hurried his fast chariot
50 To the sea Isthmos, and sent away Aiakos
Hither on golden mares,

While he went to watch over
The ridge of Korinth famous for feasting.
   But no joy will stay the same among men.
If for Melesias I have run back in my song
To the fame he wins from young athletes,
55 Let no sharp stone of hatred strike me.
I will tell, too, of this joy he won
Himself at Nemea,
And that later he fought with grown men

In the Fighting Match. (Who knows for himself
60 Will more easily teach:
Not to learn first is folly,
Since untried men have less weight to their minds.)
But here is the Master, to say beyond others
The right way for the man to go
Who would get from the holy Games
His heart's desire of glory.
Now as a gift for him
65 Alkimedon wins his thirtieth victory.

IV

God favoured him, neither
Did he lack manhood.

On the limbs of four boys he put away from him
The hateful return, the dishonouring tongue,
The secret by-path,
70 And into his father's father he breathed
Strength to resist old age.
A man forgets death when all goes well.

But I must wake Memory and tell
75 This final triumph of the hands of the Blepsiadai.
Now on their brows a sixth wreath is fastened
From the leaf-garlanded Games.
Dead men also have a part
In rites lawfully done,
Nor does the dust hide from them
80 Their kinsmen's fond delight.

Iphion has listened to Hermes' daughter,
Good-Tidings, and will tell Kallimachos
Of the bright ornament at Olympia
Which Zeus gave to their race.
85 May he consent to give good upon good
And keep away the stabs of sickness.
I pray that in bestowing glory
He will not let Doom waver in purpose,
But bring a life without sorrow
And strengthen them and their city.

Olympian VIII was composed in 460 B.C.

20 Aigina was at this time being attacked by Athens.

28 He expresses his anxiety for the future of Aigina.

30–46 The myth tells how Aiakos helped Poseidon and Apollo to build Troy, and an omen of its future was seen in the behaviour of three snakes.

45 The first generation is Aiakos. His sons Telamon and Peleus fight

with Herakles against Troy. Their sons, Aias and Achilles, make the third generation. The fourth is Neoptolemos.

47 Xanthos is a Lykian river; Ister possibly the Danube.

51 'Hither', to Aigina.

53 Melesias, already mentioned in *Nemean VI*, is being attacked as an Athenian, and his employers almost for co-operating with the national enemy.

66 Alkimedon's victory is the thirtieth won by a pupil of Melesias.

69 Pindar has no consolation to offer to the unsuccessful competitors.

77 The news of the boy's victory reaches his dead father, Iphion, and Kallimachos, his dead uncle.

NEMEAN VIII

For Deinias of Aigina, winner in the double foot-race

I

Lady Youth, herald
Of Aphrodita's celestial loves,
Seated on the eyelids of girls and boys,
One you lift with gentle hands of compulsion,
Another with different touch.
In every action the heart
Desires not to stray from the right moment
5 But to have power to win the nobler loves,

Such as waited upon the bed of Zeus and Aigina,
And brought the Cyprian's gifts to the fold.
A son was born, king of the Vineland,
Foremost in hand and in counsel.
Many men often prayed to look on his face:
Unbidden the finest heroes around
10 Wished to choose and obey his dominion,

Both those who in rocky Athens hammered an army to-
      gether,
And Pelops' sons in Sparta.
I cling to Aiakos' knees in prayer
For his dear city and for these citizens,
15 And bring a Lydian scarf embroidered with ringing bells.
An ornament from Nemea for two races on foot,
Which Deinias and his father Megas won.
When a god has helped its planting
Happiness stays longer with men;

II

Such as once loaded with wealth
Kinyras in sea-girt Kypros. I stand on feet lightly poised
And take a deep breath before speaking.
20 Much has been said in many a way;
To find new themes
And put them to the touchstone for proof
Is nothing but danger. Words
Sharpen the appetite of envy,
Which clings always to the noble
And struggles not against the base.

It put its teeth into Telamon's son,
And rolled him onto his sword.
A man without words but noble in heart
25 Oblivion hides in ugly strife;
And the greatest prize has been handed to slippery false-
hood.
For in privy ballot
The Danaoi favoured Odysseus,
And Aias, robbed of the golden armour,
Came to grips with death.

Unequal indeed were the wounds they tore
In the warm flesh of their adversaries
30 With succouring spears, hard pressed,
Some over Achilles newly slain,
And in other tasks in days of huge slaughter.
– Of old too was hateful trickery;
She walked with wheedling words and plotted death,
Slander who works evil;
She does violence to glory
And sets up a flimsy fame for the unknown.

III

35 Father Zeus, may such a temper never be mine,
But may I keep to plain paths of life,
And when I die,
Leave to my children a name
Of which no evil is spoken.
Men pray for gold, others for boundless land,
But I to please my townsmen,
Till I wrap my limbs in earth,
Praising what should be praised,
And scattering reproach on wrongdoers.

40 Prowess swells as a shoot of the vine
With fresh dews,
Lifted on high among the wise and the good among men
To the liquid sky. Manifold are the uses
Of friends. Help in trouble
Is highest, but delight also seeks
To set its truth before their eyes.
— Megas, to call your life back again

45 I am not able. Hopes are empty, and vain their end.
But it is a light task
To support your land and the Chariadai
On a stone of the Muses,
In honour of two men's running twice fortunate. I am
    glad
To utter fit praise of what has been done,
50 And by songs a man takes the pain out of toil.
    In truth of old was a triumph-song
Even before the quarrel began
Between Adrastos and the Sons of Kadmos.

Nemean VIII was written about 459 B.C.
8 The son is Aiakos.

18 For Kinyras see *Pythian II*, 15.

23–34 The suicide of Aias is an example of what slander can drive a man to do.

44 Megas is the dead father of Deinias.

50–51 The last lines seem to mean no more than that song has always been a reward and consolation to men. In the present case war between Aigina and Athens may be in the offing, and song is needed as much as ever.

PYTHIAN XI

For Thrasydaios of Thebes, winner in the boys' foot-race

I

Daughters of Kadmos,
Semela, neighbour
Of the mistresses of Olympos,
And Ino, White Goddess,
Sharer of the Nereids' sea-chambers,
Come with the mother of Herakles
(Blessed was her womb)
To Melia's presence, where the gold tripods stand
Inviolate in the Treasury,
5   That Loxias honoured before all,

And named it Ismenion, faithful seat
Of prophecy, O children of Harmonia,
Where now he bids assemble together
The folk that inhabits the Princesses' land,
Come here and sing aloud
Of holy Themis and Pytho
And the straight justice of the navel of the world,
10   When the evening has come,

Giving beauty to seven-gated Thebes
And to the course at Krisa, where Thrasydaios
Renowned the hearth of his fathers
And cast on it a third crown,
15   Triumphing in the rich ploughlands of Pyladas,
The friend of Spartan Orestas:

II

Whom Arsinoa, his nurse,
After his father's murder at the strong hands
Of Klytaimestra,
Saved from that grievous traitress, whose grey bronze
20 Made Kassandra, Dardanid Priam's child,
Bear company with Agamemnon's spirit
To Acheron's shadowy shore,

Pitiless woman. Was it Iphigeneia,
Slain at Euripos far from her land,
That stung her to uplift
The wrath of her heavy hand?
Or was she broken in to a paramour's bed
25 And the nightly loves
Turned her mind? That sin in young wives
None forgives,
And there is no way to hide it,

For others will talk,
And foul speech runs in a city.
For bliss makes envy as big as itself;
30 And he who breathes the dust
Whispers, but is not known.
    And the son of Atreus himself, the hero,
Died, when with years he returned,
In famous Amyklai.

III

And brought death on the maiden prophetess, he
Who had burned for Helen's sake
The Trojans' houses, and made cease their delight.
And Orestas the young child
35 Came to a friend, old Strophios, who dwelt

At the foot of Parnassos. Yet Ares at the last
Brought him to slay his mother, and lay Aigisthos in
    blood.

– My friends, I have been in confusion
At the crossroads where the ways divide
Though I went on a straight path before.
Has a gale thrown me
40 Out of my course like a boat at sea?
– Muse, you have made a bargain to hire
Your tongue for silver
And have got to keep it agog, now here, now there,

For Pythonikos today
Or Thrasydaios his son. Behold
45 The fire of their mirth and glory!
Proud chariot-victors of old
At the famed Olympic contest, with their horses
They won that lightning splendour,

IV

And at Pytho they entered the naked lists
50 And foiled the hosted Hellenes with their swiftness.
    God help me to love beauty, yet desire
What I may have, among men of my age.
Having seen that the middle fortune in a city
Abounds longer in bliss, I have no use
For the state of tyrants.

I have put my strength
To achievements that all share, but envious men
Are kept away.
55 He that has found those heights
And by living in quietness there
Has escaped devilish presumption,

Comes to a verge more beautiful
Than black death, if to his children,
His sweet joy, he leaves
The best of his treasures,
A good and well-loved name;

Such as carries about in song
60 Iolaos, Iphikles' son,
And strong Kastor, and you, prince Polydeukes,
You sons of Gods,
Who dwell, one day, in graves below Therapna,
And Olympos holds you on the morrow.

Pythian XI is variously said by the ancient commentators to have been composed in 474 B.C., and in 454 B.C. The latter seems more likely, and the background is the conquest of Boiotia in the autumn of that year by Athens. The song seems to have been sung at Thebes in the following spring.

4–5 The festival is held at night in honour of Theban heroines. Melia was a nymph who bore a son to Apollo and was honoured in the Ismenion.

7 Harmonia is the wife of Kadmos.

10 Delphoi was thought to be the centre of the earth; the navel was a primitive stone presumed to be the actual centre.

14 Victories have been won by the father and before him by an unnamed forebear at Delphoi.

15 Though the transition to the myth looks entirely superficial, the myth itself demonstrates that in due course the gods punish the wicked. In this we may see a forecast that Athens will in time be expelled from Boiotia, as indeed she was in 447 B.C.

17–37 The myth of the vengeance taken by Orestas on Klytaimestra for her murder of his father. Pindar's version differs from those of the tragedians.

17 Arsinoa is Orestas' nurse.

32 In other accounts the murder took place in Mykenai or Argos.

38 ff. Pindar moves abruptly away from the myth to speak of the family.

41–2 Pindar certainly seems to be paid for his work. See *Isthmian II*.

46 The Olympian victory is at some time in the past.

51 ff. Pindar has been accused of some political misdemeanour, perhaps of having relations with the pro-Athenian governors of Boiotia. He disclaims anything of the kind.

53 The 'state of tyrants' refers to the present kind of government.

59–64 The close association of the Theban hero Iolaos and the Spartan heroes, the Dioskouroi, suggests that Pindar sees the liberation of Thebes as depending on her co-operation with Sparta.

ISTHMIAN VII

For Strepsiadas of Thebes, winner in the Trial of Strength

I

In which of your land's past glories,
O happy Theba,
Have you most delighted your heart?
Was it when you exalted Dionysos with flowing hair
5 To sit beside Damater for whom the brass rings,
Or when at midnight
You welcomed the greatest of Gods
In a shower of gold,

When he stood at Amphitryon's doorway
And sought his wife for the begetting of Herakles?
Or in Teiresias' subtle counsels?
Or in Iolaos' skilled horsemanship?
10 Or in the unwearying spears of the Sown Men? Or when
You sent Adrastos from the violent battle-cry,

Widowed of countless companions,
To Argos city of horses?
Or set upright on steady ankle
The Dorian colony of Lakedaimonians,
15 And the Sons of Aigeus, your descendants,
Took Amyklai by oracles from Pytho?
    But ancient beauty slumbers, and men forget

II

Whatever has not been yoked to echoing streams of song
To come to the topmost peak of art.

20 Revel then with the hymn's sweet notes
And with Strepsiadas. For at the Isthmos he wins
Victory in the Trial of Strength.
His strength is wonderful, and to behold
He is beautiful. He wins success
That brings no shame to his breeding.

He is aflame with the violet-crowned Muses,
And has given a share of their blossoms
To his uncle who shares his name,
25 For whom bronze-shielded Ares mingled doom;
But honour is laid up for the brave.
Let him know this clearly, whosoever
In this cloud keeps off the hail of blood
From the country which he loves,

Who pays back havoc to a host of enemies,
And swells a huge glory for the race of his townsmen,
30 In life and in death.
You, son of Diodotos, matched
The warrior Meleagros, and matched
Hektor and Amphiaraos,
When you breathed out your youth in all its flower-time

III

35 In the foremost press of the fighters,
Where the bravest kept up the struggle of battle
In desperate hopes.
I suffered grief not to be spoken of. But now
The Earth-Holder has granted me calm
After the storm. I shall fasten garlands on my hair
And sing, and may the envy of Immortals not trouble me.

I shall seek the delight that each day brings
And in calm of mind

Come to old age and my fated days;
For all alike we die,
Though our doom is unequal.
If a man peers at what is afar,
He is too small to reach
The bronze-floored home of the Gods.
Winged Pagasos threw off

His master Bellerophon
When he wished to come to the sky's dwellings
And the company of Zeus.
A most bitter end
Awaits what is sweet in despite of right.
    Do thou, Loxias, with thy blossom of golden hair,
Grant in thy contests
A crown of fine flowers to us at Pytho also.

Isthmian VII was probably composed about 454 B.C. after the battle of
Oinophyta, in which the Athenians became masters of Boiotia.

3 The ringing brass concerns Damater in connexion with the mysteries.

5–7 Zeus, taking the shape of Amphitryon, begat Herakles from
Alkmana.

8 Teiresias is the famous prophet. See *Nemean I*.

9 Iolaos, the Theban, is the close companion of Herakles.

11 Adrastos, one of the Seven against Thebes, is repulsed in battle.

27–37 The victor's uncle, Strepsiadas, has been killed at Oinophyta, and
is compared with heroes of the past.

43–8 When Bellerophon on Pagasos tried to come to Olympos, it
threw him. See *Olympian XIII*, 91–2. This probably hints at Athens,
which will come to disaster for wanting too much.

OLYMPIAN IV

For Psaumis of Kamarina, winner in the chariot-race

Charioteer most high
Of the unweary-footed lightning,
Zeus, thy circling Hours have sent me
With the gamut of the harp's song
5 To witness the loftiest of Games.
When friends fare well,
Straightway at the sweet news
Good men are glad.
   Son of Kronos, master of windy Aitna,
Where powerful Typhos is trapped,
The hundred-headed,
10 Welcome an Olympian conqueror,
And, for the Graces' sake, this procession,

A light most lasting on deeds of great strength.
For Psaumis comes
On his chariot, crowned with the olive of Pisa.
15 He is eager to set up renown
For Kamarina. May God be kind
To his prayers in time to come.
For I praise him, ready indeed to train horses,
Glad to entertain all strangers,
With his pure heart turned
20 To Quiet who loves his city.
With no lie shall I stain the saying:
'Trial is the test of men.'

– This freed Klymenos' son
25 From the Lemnian women's disdain.

When he won the race in bronze armour,
He said to Hypsipyleia,
As he came to get his crown:
'Such am I in fastness of foot:
My hand and my heart are to match.
Even on young men white hair grows
30   Before the due season of life.'

Olympian IV was composed in 452 B.C. Nothing is known of Psaumis except that he was rather past the usual age for competing in the Games.

24–30 Klymenos' son is the Argonaut Erginos, who won in the race in armour, over which Hypsipyleia, queen of the Amazons, presided.

NEMEAN XI

For Aristagoras of Tenedos, on his presentation
at the Council Hall

I

Daughter of Rhea, to you the Council Hall belongs,
Hestia, sister of highest Zeus
And of Hera who shares his throne,
Receive Aristagoras gladly into your chamber,
And gladly his companions
Near to your shining sceptre;
5   – They honour you and keep Tenedos upright.

They worship the first of goddesses
Often with libations, often with incense.
For them the harp rings loud, and the song;
And Right is practised by them at the never-failing board
Of Zeus the strangers' God.
– May he pass to the end of his twelve months' task
10   In good repute with heart unwounded.

As for the man, I count him happy
For his father Hagesilas
And for his own marvellous body
And the fearlessness born with him.
But if any is fortunate
And likely to surpass others in beauty
And has shown his strength by being best in the Games,
15   Let him remember: the limbs that he clothes are mortal
And at the end of all he will put on a garment of
   clay.

II

It is right that he should be praised
With good words from his townsmen,
And decked with sweet-sounding songs for men to sing.
Sixteen shining victories,
Won from the dwellers around,
20 Have crowned Aristagoras and his fortunate country
In wrestling and the glorious Trial of Strength.

The timorous hopes of his parents held back their strong
    son
From trying the Games at Pytho and Olympia.
I say it on oath, in my belief,
If he had gone to Kastalia
25 And to Kronos' well-wooded hill,
He would have come home with more glory
Than the adversaries who fought him.

In the fifth-year festival founded by Herakles
He would have joined the revel and tied his hair
With purple branches. But among men
30 One is flung from success by empty-hearted boasts,
But another, who rates too poorly his strength,
Lets the honours within his reach
Slip from his hand,
Plucked back by his unadventurous heart.

III

It were easy to guess in him
The ancient blood of Peisandros from Sparta,
– From Amyklai he came with Orestas
35 And brought hither a troop of Aeolians armoured in
    bronze –
And Ismenos' water flows in his veins

Through Melanippos his mother's father.
High ancient enterprises

Renew their strength for the generations of men
In alternate ages.
Black ploughlands give not fruit in unbroken succession,
40 And trees consent not in every year
To bear sweet-scented flowers in equal abundance,
But in each second season.
So is the human race driven

By fate. Of what comes from Zeus
We have no sure sign, and yet
We set foot upon great endeavours
45 And hanker for many things.
Our bodies are chained to wanton hope,
And the waters of foresight lie far away.
We must hunt for the mean in our profits –
Loves beyond reach sting too sharply to madness.

Nemean XI is not a true Epinician but a song to celebrate the admission of the young Aristagoras to a post in the local council hall, as a cup-bearer or something of the kind. The poem was included among the Epinicians because of its references to the games in which Aristagoras has, or has not, taken part. It was composed late in Pindar's life, possibly about 446 B.C. Aristagoras was the brother of Theoxenos, in whose arms Pindar was said to have died at Argos.

2 Hestia, the goddess of the hearth.

24–5 If Aristagoras had competed in the Pythian and Olympian Games, he would have won.

33 Peisandros was a Spartan who came to Tenedos with Orestas and founded the Greek colony there.

37 On his mother's side the boy is descended from the Theban hero Melanippos.

47–8 Pindar may be hinting obliquely at his own love for Theoxenos, for whom at this time he wrote a poem, which survives more or less complete:

We should, my heart, gather the flowers of love
At the moment that fits our years,
But if anyone sees the flashes
That shoot from the eyes of Theoxenos
And is not rolled on a wave of desire, of adamant
Or of iron has he been forged in his black heart

By a chilling force. Unhonoured
By black-eyed Aphrodita,
Either he toils brutally for money,
Or with a woman's effrontery
He reels down every road, solacing his soul.
But I, because of the goddess, am gnawed by the heat

And melt like the wax of holy bees, whenever I look
Upon the youth and fresh limbs of boys.
Truly in Tenedos also
Attraction dwells, and Beauty
Nursed the son of Hagesilas.

PYTHIAN VIII

For Aristomenes of Aigina, winner in the boys' wrestling

I

Kind-hearted Quiet, daughter of Right,
You, who make mightiest cities
And hold the last keys of counsel or war,
Accept in the name of Aristomenes
5 This Pythian victor-song.
For to use gentleness, or to be used with it,
You know the perfect time:

You too, if any
Drives home into his heart
Unsweet anger, will harden your face
10 Against the might of your enemies, and clap
The upstart in the bilge.
– Porphyrion did not know this,
When he aroused her too far
(The gain I like best
Comes from the house of a willing giver,

15 But Force trips up
At last even the loud boaster.)
– Cilician Typhos with a hundred heads
Did not escape her,
No, nor the Giants' King.
They went down before
The thunderbolt and the arrows of Apollo:
  Who welcomed with friendly heart
20 Xenarkes' son from Krisa,
With the grass of Parnassos in his hair
And with a Dorian triumph.

II

The Graces are never far
From the island city of Righteousness,
For she has at her side
The great and famous Aiakidai.
25 Her renown is perfect from the beginning.
In many victorious contests
(Her poets say) the heroes from her breast
Stood first, and in the rush of battles:

She is bright with mortal sons also.
– I cannot stop to strike up a song,
30 With harp and liquid voice, of the whole long tale,
Lest galling surfeit come.
But this, which runs at my feet,
Which you, boy, have earned,
Let it fly, the newest of her honours,
On the wings of my skill.

In wrestling matches you go in the steps
Of your mother's brothers.
Theognetos at Olympia is not shamed by you,
Nor the victory of the enduring limbs
Of Kleitomachos at the Isthmos.
You exalt the Meidylid clan: of you was the word
Spoken in riddles once by Oikleës' son,
When he saw the Sons holding their ground
40 In the seven gates of Thebes,

III

When they came from Argos
On the second journey, the Afterborn.
Thus he spoke, whilst they fought –
'Blood makes this noble temper

45 Shine from their fathers in the sons.
   I see him clearly
   Plying the coiled snake on his fiery shield,
   Alkman, the first in the gates of Kadmos:

   But he that was broken with trouble before
50 Is compassed with better-omened news,
   The hero Adrastos;
   Though his own kin shall turn his joy to woe.
   He, and none of the Danaans beside,
   Shall gather the bones of his own dead son,
   And so by the Gods' will shall come,
   His army unharmed,

55 To the wide streets where Abas ruled.'
   So Amphiaraos spoke.
   And I too
   Am pleased to lay my wreaths upon Alkman
   And shed the dew of my song.
   He is my neighbour, he guards my goods,
   He met me in my road
   To Earth's renownèd Navel,
60 And broached that prophet's art
   Which is his by inheritance.

IV

   And you, Far-Shooter,
   Master of the glorious shrine
   Which welcomes all in the valley of Pytho,
65 You granted there that greatest of joys.
   And at home before this,
   In the feast of your Sister and you,
   You added the Fivefold Contest's coveted prize.
   My King, be pleasèd, I pray you,
   To let your eyes rain melody

On every step that I take.
70 At the side of the sweet-singing procession
Justice is standing: and I pray, Xenarkes,
For the Gods' unenvious regards
On all your fortunes.
    For many suppose, he who has won good things
With no long stretch of toil
Is the wise man among fools

75 And marshals his life
With plans of unerring judgement.
– But such things do not lie in man's power.
Fate is the giver, and throws
Now one man above, now another beneath, his hands.
Compete in measure: you have had the prize
At Megara and in the valley of Marathon.
And of those Games of Hera at your home
80 In three victories, Aristomenes,
You have made a conquest indeed.

V

And now four times you came down with bodies
        beneath you,
(You meant them harm),
To whom the Pythian feast has given
No glad home-coming like yours.
85 They, when they meet their mothers,
Have no sweet laughter around them moving delight.
In back streets out of their enemies' way,
They cower; disaster has bitten them.

But who, in his tenderest years,
Finds some new lovely thing,
His hope is high, and he flies
90 On the wings of his manhood:

Better than riches are his thoughts.
– But man's pleasure is a short time growing
And it falls to the ground
As quickly, when an unlucky twist of thought
Loosens its roots.

95 Man's life is a day. What is he?
What is he not? A shadow in a dream
Is man: but when God sheds a brightness,
Shining life is on earth
And life is sweet as honey.
      Aigina, dear mother,
Keep this city in her voyage of freedom:
You with Zeus and lord Aiakos,
100   Peleus, and noble Telamon, and Achilles.

Pythian VIII was written in 446 B.C. and performed in Aigina at a time
of great expectation and excitement when it looked as if Aigina, which
had for some ten years been under Athenian rule, might exploit Athens'
present troubles to free herself. Pindar has this situation very much in
mind and sympathizes with the eager young athlete but at the same time
instils warnings and advice.

1 The invocation of Quiet is to induce a balanced state of mind in a
time of crisis.

12 The giant Porphyrion is a type of brutal arrogance which brings its
own downfall, and to some extent a symbol for Athens which may do
the same.

17 For Typhos, see *Pythian I*, 15 ff.

39 Oikleës' son is Amphiaraos.

39–56 A short myth tells how when the Successors came to attack
Thebes, Amphiaraos foretells that Alkman (Alkmaion) will lose his son.
The point is that in any war allowance must be made in advance for
losses.

36–60 On his way from Thebes to Delphoi Pindar has seen Alkmaion,
in a vision or a dream, and heard a prophecy from him, which he does
not disclose but may refer to the success of the victor.

98–100 The heroes named with Zeus are the traditional guardians of
Aigina and will fight for her if war comes.

(OLYMPIAN V)

For Psaumis of Kamarina, winner with the mule-car

I

Of lofty triumphs the highest and sweetest
Won at Olympia, O daughter of Ocean, with smiling
heart
Welcome, and the gifts of the unweary-footed chariot
and of Psaumis:

Who honours thy town, Kamarina, nurse of its people,
5   And hallowed the six twin altars at the Gods' greatest
feast
With sacrifice of oxen and the struggle of games on five
days,
With horses and mules and the single rider. For thee
tender glory
He laid up by his victory, and he proclaimed
His father Akron and the new-built city.

II

10   Coming from the lovely precincts of Oinomaos and
Pelops,
O Pallas, supporter of cities, he sings of the holy grove,
Thy river, Oanis, and the pools of the land,
And the hallowed channels, with which Hipparis waters
thy host,
And welds swiftly together the high-limbed avenue of
well-built halls,
15   Bringing this people of citizens from perplexity to light.
Even in noble causes the toil and the cost contend

Against a task wrapped in danger.
But if men prosper, their townsmen think them wise.

III

O saviour Zeus in the clouds, dweller on Kronos' Hill,
20 Who honourest Alpheos' broad stream and Ida's holy
    cave,
    Suppliant to thee I come to the strain of Lydian flutes,

To ask thee to deck the city with renowned manhood,
And thou, Olympian conqueror, delighting in Poseidon's
    mares,
Mayest thou carry to the end a high-hearted old age,

25 Psaumis, with sons at thy side. If a man waters healthy
    happiness,
    Content with his possessions
    And adding glory to them, let him not seek to be God.

Olympian V is almost certainly not the work of Pindar but was added to his works by the Alexandrian scholar Didymos in the first century B.C. It looks like the work of a Sicilian imitator, writing for the same Psaumis as Pindar celebrated in *Olympian IV*, to be sung on his return to Kamarina, probably in 448 B.C. The poem follows a strict plan. Each triad is complete, the first addressed to the nymph Kamarina, the second to Pallas, the third to Zeus, and this may mean that the song was performed in a procession which halted at three stations.

2 Kamarina is a daughter of Ocean.

5 The six twin-altars at Olympia was where successful athletes sacrificed.

12 Oanis is a river of Kamarina.

13 So too is Hipparis.

14 The meaning is much disputed. The words may refer to timber brought down the river for building, or to bricks baked from its mud. Neither is very convincing.

20 The cave of Ida seems to have been on the Hill of Kronos at Olympia.

REGISTER OF NAMES

m = mythical

m Abas, king of Argos, son of Lynkeus and father of Talaos.

Achaioi, Greeks living variously in Thessaly, Peloponnese, and Epirus.

Acharnai, country district of Attica.

Acheron, river of the underworld.

m Achilles, son of Peleus and Thetis.

m Admatos, son of Pheras and kinsman of Jason.

m Adrastos, son of Talaos, king of Argos, and one of the Seven against Thebes.

Aegis-holder, Zeus.

m Agamemnon, king of Argos, murdered by his wife Klytaimestra, father of Orestas.

m Aiakos, son of Zeus and Aigina, ancestor of the Aiakidai.

m Aias, son of Telamon, fights at Troy, kills himself on not being awarded the armour of the dead Achilles.

m Aias, son of Ileus, hero, fought at Troy.

m Aietas, king of Kolchis and father of Medeia.

Aigai, seat of Poseidon in Achaia.

Aigeidai, famous clan with branches in several Greek cities. Pindar and King Arkesilas IV of Kyrene both belonged to it.

m Aigimios, Dorian king, father of Pamphylos.

m Aigisthos, paramour of Klytaimestra and murderer of Agamemnon, himself killed by Orestas.

Aineas, leader of the choir which celebrates Hagesias.

Ainesidamos, of Akragas, father of Theron and Xenokrates.

m Aiolos, son of Helen and father of Sisyphos, gives name to Aiolidai or Aeolians.

m Aipytos, son of Elatus, king of Phaisana in Arkadia and father of Evadna.

m Aison, son of Kretheus and king of part of Thessaly, father of Jason.

Aitna, volcano in Sicily, under which the giant Typhos was
believed to be buried. Also town founded by Hieron on its
slope.

m Akastos, son of Pelias, king of Iolkos and Magnesia, husband of
Hippolyta.

Akragas, city on southern coast of Sicily.

m Aktor, father of Menoitios and grandfather of Patroklos.

m Alatas, descendant of Herakles and founder of Korinth.

Alektran Gates, at Thebes, looking towards Plataia.

Aleuas, Thessalian prince, father of Thorax, Eurypylos, and
Thrasydaios.

Alexibiadas, Karrhotos, charioteer of King Arkesilas IV.

Alexidamos, distant ancestor of Telesikrates of Kyrene.

m Alkaios, grandfather of Herakles.

m Alkathoos, son of Pelops and founder of Games at Megara.

Alkimedon, Aiginetan, son of Iphion and member of the family of
Blepsiadai.

Alkimidas, Aiginetan wrestler, son of Theon.

m Alkmaion, son of Amphiaraos.

Alkmaionidai, famous Athenian family, of which Megakles was a
member.

m Alkmana, wife of Amphitryon and mother of Herakles and
Iphikles.

m Alkyoneus, giant killed by Herakles and Telamon.

Alpheos, river at Olympia, passes under sea to reappear at Syracuse
as the fountain Arethoisa.

Altis, sacred grove at Olympia.

m Amazons, women warriors living by the river Thermodon.

Amenas, river of Sicily watering Katana by Aitna.

Ammon, name by which Zeus is worshipped in Africa.

m Amphiaraos, son of Oikleës, king of Argos, one of the Seven
against Thebes.

Amyklai, city of the Peloponnese captured by the Dorians under
Herakles.

m Amyntor, father of Astydameia and grandfather of Tlapolemos.

m Amythaon, son of Kretheus and brother of Aison, an Argonaut.

m Antaios, king of Libya, who could not be defeated so long as he kept his feet on the ground. Herakles lifted him and killed him.

m Antenor, Trojan, father of the first founders of Kyrene.
     Antias, noble Argive.

m Antilochos, son of Nestor, for whom he gave his life.

m Aphareus, father of Idas and Lynkeus.
     Aphrodita, goddess of love. Also called Kypris (the Cyprian).
     Apollo, god of song and prophecy, with seats at Delphoi and Delos, also called Phoibos.
     Archestratos, of Western Lokroi, father of the athlete Hagesidamos.
     Archilochos, poet of the seventh century, renowned for his sharp tongue.
     Area's Ford, on eastern coast of Sicily.
     Ares, god of war.
     Arethoisa, fountain in Syracuse.

m Argo, ship of the Argonauts in the quest for the Golden Fleece.
     Argos, city of the north-eastern Peloponnese.
     Aristagoras, of Tenedos, son of Hagesilas.
     Aristaios, son of Apollo and Kyrene, god of the countryside.
     Aristodemos, Argive remembered for a single remark.
     Aristokleidas, Aiginetan, son of Aristophanes, athlete.
     Aristomenes, Aiginetan boy athlete, son of Xenarkes.
     Aristophanes, Aiginetan, father of the athlete Aristokleidas.
     Aristoteles, another name for Battos, the founder of Kyrene.
     Arkadia, central, mountainous region of the Peloponnese.
     Arkesilas IV, king of Kyrene.

m Arsinoa, nurse of Orestas, saves his life in childhood.
     Artemis, goddess, twin sister of Apollo.

m Asklapios, son of Apollo and Koronis, later god of healing.
     Asopichos, of Orchomenos, boy athlete, son of Kleodamos.
     Asopodoros, of Thebes, father of the chariot-racer Herodotos.
     Asopos, river of Boiotia and of Sikyon, father of cities.

m Astydameia, daughter of Amyntor and mother of Tlapolemos.
     Atabyrion, mountain in central Rhodes.
     Athana, goddess, also called Pallas.

m Atlas, a Titan, supports the sky on his shoulders.

m Atreus, son of Pelops and father of Agamemnon.

m Augeas, king of the Epeians, killed by Herakles.

Bassidai, Aiginetan family.

Battos, first king of Kyrene, previously called Aristoteles.

m Bellerophon, Korinthian hero, son of Glaukos and grandson of Sisyphos, rides on Pagasos.

Blepsiadai, noble Aiginetan family.

Boibias, Thessalian lake.

Bright-eyed One, Athana.

Chariadai, Aiginetan family.

m Chariklo, wife of Cheiron.

m Cheiron, centaur, son of Kronos and Philyra.

m Chimaira, monster killed by Bellerophon.

Chromios, Syracusan soldier.

m Daidalos, Cretan craftsman.

Damagetos, Rhodian, father of the athlete Diagoras.

Damater, goddess of crops.

Damophilos, leader of opposition in Kyrene and friend of Pindar.

m Danaä, mother of Perseus.

m Danaoi, synonym for Greeks who fought at Troy.

m Dardanoi, Trojans.

m Dardanos, Troy.

Deinias, Aiginetan boy athlete, son of Megas.

Deinomenes, father of Hieron and titular king of Aitna.

Delos, island in Aegean, birthplace of Apollo and Artemis.

Delphoi, on slope of Parnassos, seat of Apollo's oracle and the Pythian Games.

m Deukalion, husband of Pyrrha, with her forms the first human couple after the great flood.

Diagoras, Rhodian athlete, son of Damagetos.

Diodotos, Theban, father of the elder Strepsiadas and grandfather of the young athlete of the same name.

m Diomedes, Argive hero.

Dionysos, god of wine and ecstasy.

m Dioskouroi, twin sons of Leda – Kastor and Polydeukes.
   Dirka, fountain at Thebes.
   Dodona, seat of oracle of Zeus in north-west Greece.
m Doryklos, from Tiryns, competitor at first Olympian Games.

m Echemos, from Tegea, winner in the first Olympian Games.
m Echion, son of Hermes and Antianeira, an Argonaut.
   Elatos, father of Aipytos (Eilatidas).
   Eleithyia, birth-goddess.
   Eleusis, outside Athens, seat of Eleusinian Games.
   Emmenidai, family at Akragas, descended from Emmenis and
      ultimately from Polyneikes.
m Endaïs, daughter of Cheiron, wife of Aiakos, and mother of
      Peleus and Telamon.
m Epaphos, son of Io, king of Libya and forebear of Aigyptos and
      Danaos.
m Epeians, people of Elis, ruled by Augeas.
   Epharmostos, wrestler, member of ancient family in Opous.
m Ephialtas, son of Poseidon and Iphimedeia, of gigantic stature.
   Ephyra, ancient capital of Thesprotia, where the Acheron flows
      into the sea.
   Epidauros, Argive district near Saronic Gulf, where games were
      held in honour of Asklapios.
   Eratidai, Rhodian family, descended from Tlapolemos, son of
      Herakles.
m Erechtheus, mythical king of Athens.
   Ergoteles, Cretan athlete from Knossos, exiled to Himera.
m Eriboia, daughter of Alkathoos, wife of Telamon, mother of
      Aias.
   Eriphyla, wife of Amphiaraos.
   Eritimos, Korinthian athlete, brother of Terpsias.
m Erytos, son of Hermes and Antianeira, an Argonaut.
   Euboia, large island east of Attica.
m Euphamos, son of Poseidon, an Argonaut.
   Euphanes, Aiginetan, father of Kallikles and grandfather of
      Timasarchos.
   Euripos, tidal strait between Euboia and Chalkis.

m Europa, daughter of Tityos.
  Eurotas, river of Sparta.
m Euryala, a Gorgon, killed by Perseus.
m Eurypylos, demigod, son of Poseidon and Kelaino.
m Eurystheus, king of Argos, half-brother of Herakles.
m Eurytos, one of the Moliones, killed by Herakles.
m Evadna, daughter of Poseidon and Pitana, mother of Iamos.

  Gadeira, city in Spain, regarded as the limit of the known world.
m Ganymedes, Trojan boy, carried off by Zeus to be his cup-
    bearer.
m Geryon, giant with three heads, in Spain, killed by Herakles.
m Glaukos, son of Hippolochos, hero from Lykia in Trojan War.
  Golden-haired, the, Apollo.
m Gorgons, monsters, daughters of Phorkos.

  Hagesias, son of Sostratos, Syracusan, victor with mule-car.
  Hagesidamos, 1. from Western Lokroi, boy boxer, son of
    Archestratos.
  Hagesidamos, 2. father of Chromios of Aitna.
  Hagesilas, of Tenedos, father of Aristagoras.
m Haimones, Thessalian tribe.
m Halirrothios, of Mantinea, father of Samos.
m Hektor, Trojan hero, son of Priam.
m Helen, daughter of Zeus and Leda, wife first of Menelaos, then of
    Paris.
m Helenos, son of Priam.
  Helikonian maidens, the Muses.
  Hellas, Greece.
  Hellotian Games, at Korinth.
  Heloros, river of Sicily.
  Hermes, messenger of the gods and patron of games.
  Hieron, king of Syracuse.
m Hippodameia, daughter of Oinomaos and wife of Pelops.
  Hippokleas, Thessalian boy athlete, son of Phrikias.
m Hippolyta, daughter of Kretheus and wife of Akastos.
m Hyperboreans, mythical people living beyond the North wind.

Hypereïs, fountain near Pherai in Thessaly.

Hyperion's child, the Sun.

m Hypermestra, daughter of Danaos of Argos and wife of Lynkeus, whom she refused to kill when all her sisters killed their husbands.

m Hypseus, son of Kretheus and Kreoisa, king of the Lapiths.

m Hypsipyleia, queen of the Amazons.

m Ialysos, legendary Rhodian, son of Kerkaphos and grandson of the Sun, eponymous hero of city with the same name.

m Iamos, legendary founder of the clan of Iamids, son of Apollo and Evadna.

m Iapetos, founder of a family in Opous.

m Idas, son of Aphareus, legendary king of Messenia.

m Ilas, trainer of Hagesidamos.

m Ino, daughter of Kadmos.

m Iolaos, companion of Herakles, son of Iphikles.

Iolkos, city in Thessaly.

Ionian Sea, between Greece and Thessaly.

m Iphigeneia, daughter of Agamemnon and Klytaimestra.

m Iphikles, twin brother of Herakles.

Iphion, Aiginetan, father of athlete Alkimedon.

Irasa, city of Libya.

Ismenos, river of Thebes.

Ismenion, temple of Apollo on bank of the above.

Ister, ancient name for the Danube.

Isthmus, of Korinth, joining the Peloponnese to mainland.

m Ixion, first man to commit bloodshed; also assaulted Hera.

m Jason, son of Aison, leader of the Argonauts.

Kadmeians, Thebans.

m Kadmos, son of Agenor, founder of Thebes.

Kaïkos, river of Mysia.

m Kalaïs, winged son of Boreas.

Kallianax, Rhodian, ancestor of Diagoras.

Kallias, Aiginetan boxer.

Kallikles, Aiginetan, uncle of Timasarchos, son of Euphanes.

Kallimachos, Aiginetan, dead kinsman of Alkimedon.

m Kamiros, legendary Rhodian, son of Kerkaphos and grandson of the Sun and Rhodes, eponymous hero of city with the same name.

Kaphisos, river flowing through Boiotia and Phokis.

Karneiadas, of Kyrene, father of Telesikrates.

Karrhotos, charioteer of king Arkesilas of Kyrene; son of Alexibios.

m Kassandra, Trojan prophetess murdered by Klytaimestra.

Kastalia, fountain at Delphi.

m Kastor, son of Leda and mortal father, Tyndareos.

Keos, island off the south-east coast of Attica.

m Kinyras, king in Cyprus, loved by Aphrodite and Apollo.

Kirrha, town in valley below Delphoi, where the Pythian chariot races were held.

Kithairon, mountain of Boiotia.

Kleandros, Aiginetan boy athlete, son of Telesarchos.

Kleio, Muse.

Kleitomachos, Aiginetan, uncle of Aristomenes.

Kleitor, Arkadian town.

Kleodamos, of Orchomenos, father of Asopichos.

Kleonai, Argive city between Argos and Korinth.

Kleonikos, Aiginetan, father of Lampon.

Kleonymos, founder of a Theban clan.

Klotho, a Fate.

m Klymenos, father of Erginus.

m Klytaimestra, wife of Agamemnon.

Knossos, city of Crete.

Koiranidas, descendant of the Argive Melampos.

Kolchians, people of the eastern shore of the Black Sea.

Korinth, city of north-east Peloponnese.

m Koronis, daughter of Phlegyas, loved by Apollo, mother of Asklapios.

m Kreoisa, nymph.

Kreontidas, Aiginetan athlete.

m Kretheus, son of Aiolos and Enereia and father of Hippolyta.

Kroisos, king of Lydia.

Kronos, father of Zeus; hence Kronidas, for Zeus.

m Kteatos, one of the Moliones, brother of Eurytos, killed by Herakles.

m Kyknos, 'the Swan', legendary son of Poseidon.

Kyllana, Arkadian mountain.

Kyrene, city of northern Africa.

Labdakidai, Thebans.

Lachesis, a Fate.

m Laios, of Thebes, father of Oidipous.

Lakedaimon, Sparta.

Lakereia, city of Thessaly.

Lampon, Aiginetan athlete, of the family of the Psalychidai, son of Kleonikos, father of Pytheas and Phylakidas.

Lampromachos, of Opous, kinsman of Epharmostos.

m Laomedon, king of Troy, father of Priam.

m Lapiths, Thessalian tribe.

m Lato, bride of Zeus and mother of Apollo and Artemis.

m Leda, bride of Zeus, mother of Kastor and Polydeukes.

Lemnos, island in north-eastern Aegean.

Lerna, in the Argolis, home of the hydra.

m Leukothea, daughter of Kadmos.

Libya, land in northern Africa.

m Likymnios, son of Electryon and Midea.

m Lindos, son of Kerkaphos and grandson of the Sun and Rhodes. Also Rhodian city called after him.

Lokroi, region in central Greece.

m Lokros, king of the Opountians, husband of Protogeneia.

Loxias, Apollo.

Lykaios, title of Zeus in Arkadia.

Lykia, region in southern Asia Minor.

Magnesia, district of Thessaly.

Mainalian Hills, in Arcadia.

Mantinea, city of Arkadia.

Marathon, on east coast of Attica.

m Medeia, daughter of Aietas and wife of Jason.
m Medoisa, one of the Gorgons.
  Megakles, Athenian, member of the Alkmaionid family.
  Megara, city north of the Isthmus of Korinth.
  Megas, Aiginetan athlete, father of Deinias.
  Meidylidai, Aiginetan family.
m Melampos, son of Amythaon, an Argonaut.
m Melanippos, son of Astakis, a Theban hero.
m Meleagros, son of Oineus and Althaia, a hero.
  Melesias, Athenian trainer of athletes.
m Melia, heroine, daughter of Ocean, honoured at Thebes.
  Melissos, Theban athlete, son of Telesiadas, of the family of the
    Kleonymidai.
m Memnon, king of the Ethiopians, son of the Dawn, killed by
    Achilles.
  Menandros, trainer from Athens.
m Menelaos, brother of Agamemnon and first husband of Helen.
m Menoitios, father of Patroklos.
m Metopa, daughter of the Arkadian river Ladon and mother of
    Theba.
  Midas, flute-player from Akragas.
m Midea, mother of Likymnios.
  Minyai, ancient inhabitants of Orchomenos.
m Moliones, Kteatos and Eurytos, sons of Poseidon and Aktor.
  Molossia, district in north-west Greece.
m Mopsos, seer and Argonaut.
m Myrmidons, followers of Achilles.
  Mysian Plain, near Troy.

  Nemea, in the Argolid between Kleonai and Phleious, where
    Nemean Games were held in alternate years.
m Neoptolemos, son of Achilles.
m Nereus, sea-god, father of Thetis.
m Nestor, king of Pylos.
  Nikasippos, Sicilian charioteer.
m Nikeus, thrower of discus in first Olympian Games.
  Nikokleës, Aiginetan, kinsman of Kleandros, killed at Salamis.

Nikomachos, charioteer of Xenokrates.
m Nisos, son of Pandion, king of Megara.

m Odysseus, legendary hero.
m Oidipous, son of Laios, father of Eteokles and Polyneikes.
m Oikleës, father of Amphiaraos.
   Oineidai, descendants of Oineus, the father of Meleagros and Deianira.
m Oinomaos, legendary king of Pisa, father of Hippodameia.
m Oionos, grandson of Midea, son of Likymnios, winner of foot-race in first Olympian Games.
   Oligaithos, sons of, noble clan at Korinth.
   Olympia, in Elis on river Alpheos, scene of Olympian Games every fourth year.
   Olympos, mountain in north-east Greece and alleged home of the gods.
   Onchestos, Boiotian city.
   Opoeis, 1. legendary king of Elis.
   Opoeis, 2. Lokrian city.
   Orchomenos, Boiotian city.
m Orestas, son of Agamemnon and Klytaimestra.
m Orion, legendary hunter, turned into constellation.
m Orpheus, singer and musician.
   Orseas, trainer of Melissos.
   Ortygia, eastern part of the city of Syracuse, formerly an island.
m Otos, son of Poseidon and Iphimedeia.
   Oulias, of Argos, father of Theaios.
   Ouranidas, Kronos, son of Ouranos.

m Pagasos, winged horse of Bellerophon.
   Paian, Apollo
   Palion, mountain in Thessaly.
   Pallas, Athana.
   Pamphaes, Argive ancestor of Theaios.
   Pamphylos, son of Aigimios, founder of the Spartan state.
   Pan, god.

m Paris, son of Priam and second husband of Helen.
Parnassos, mountain above Delphoi.
m Patroklos, son of Menoitios and friend of Achilles.
Peirana, fountain in Korinth.
Peisandros, remote ancestor of Aristagoras of Tenedos, coming
    originally from Sparta.
Pellanna, town in Arkadia.
m Peleus, son of Aiakos, wife of Thetis, father of Achilles.
m Pelias, son of Poseidon (or Kretheus) and Tyro, king of Iolkos.
Pelinna, town in Thessaly.
m Pelops, son of Tantalos and founder of Olympian festival.
Peneios, Thessalian river.
Pergamos, Troy.
m Periklymenos, son of Poseidon and Chloris.
Persephona, goddess of the underworld.
m Perseus, son of Zeus and Danaä.
Phaisana, Arkadian town.
Phalaris, tyrant of Akragas.
Phasis, river of Colchis.
Pherenikos, victorious horse of Hieron.
m Pheras, brother of Aison.
m Philoktetes, hero, archer in Trojan War.
m Philyra, mother of Cheiron.
Phintis, charioteer of Hagesias.
Phlegra, on the Isthmus of Pallene, scene of battle between Gods
    and Giants.
m Phlegyas, king of the Lapiths and father of Koronis.
Phleious, Argive city.
Phoibos, Apollo.
m Phokos, Aiginetan, son of Aiakos and Psamatheia.
m Phorkos, father of the Gorgons.
m Phrastor, winner of the javelin cast at first Olympian Games.
Phrikias, Thessalian, father of Hippokleas.
m Phrixos, son of Athamas, brought to Colchis by a ram with a
    golden fleece.
Phrygians, allies of the Trojans.
Phthia, Thessalian town.

m Samos, son of Halirrothios, of Mantinea, winner of chariot-race in first Olympian Games.

m Sarpedon, son of Zeus, Lykian, fights on Trojan side.

Sekyon (Sicyon), city on north coast of Peloponnese, where games were held.

m Semela, daughter of Kadmos and mother of Dionysos.

Seriphos, island in the Aegean.

Sipylos, mountain in Asia Minor.

m Sisyphos, son of Aiolos, king of Korinth.

Skamandros, river of Troy.

Skyros, island in Aegean.

Sogenes, Aiginetan boy athlete, son of Thearion.

Solymoi, people of Asia Minor.

Sostratos, Syracusan, father of Hagesias.

Sparta, city of central Peloponnese.

m Spartoi (Sown Men), warriors sprung from the dragon's teeth.

Strepsiadas, Theban athlete.

m Strophios, king of Phokis and father of Pyladas.

Stymphalos, Arkadian city.

Tainaros, town of Lakonia near promontory of same name.

m Talaos, father of Adrastos.

m Tantalos, king of Phrygia, father of Pelops.

Tartaros, ancient Hell.

m Taÿgeta, daughter of Atlas.

Taygetos, mountain in Lakonia.

Tegea, city of Arkadia.

m Teiresias, Theban seer.

m Telamon, Aiginetan hero, father of Aias.

Teleboai, originally inhabitants of Akarnania but later migrated to various islands.

m Telephos, king of Mysia, ally of Trojans, killed by Achilles.

Telesarchos, Aiginetan, father of Kleandros.

Telesiadas, Theban, father of Melissos.

Telesikrates, of Kyrene, son of Karneiadas.

Tenedos, island off the Troad.

Terpsias, Korinthian, son of Ptoiodoros.

Terpsichora, Muse.

m Teukros, son of Telamon.

m Teuthras, king of Mysia, ally of Trojans.

Thalia, one of the Graces.

Theaios, Argive athlete.

Theandridai, Aiginetan family.

Thearion, Aiginetan, father of Sogenes.

Theba, eponymous nymph of Thebes.

Thebes, capital city of Boiotia.

Theia, goddess of light.

Themis, goddess of order.

Themistios, Aiginetan, father of Euthymenes, maternal uncle of Pytheas and Phylakidas.

Theognetos, Aiginetan, uncle of Aristomenes.

Thera, island in the Aegean.

Therapna, in Lakonia.

Theron, tyrant of Akragas, son of Ainesidamos and member of clan of Emmenidai.

Thessalos, Korinthian, son of Ptoiodoros and father of Xenophon.

Thessaly, large district in northern Greece.

m Thetis, Nereid, wife of Peleus and mother of Achilles.

Thorax, Thessalian, kinsman of Hippokleas.

Thrasyboulos, of Akragas, son of Xenokrates and nephew of Theron.

Thrasydaios, Theban boy athlete.

Thrasyklos, Argive, kinsman of Theaios.

m Thyona, Semela.

Timasarchos, Aiginetan, boy athlete, son of Timokritos.

Timodamos, from Acharnai in Attica, son of Timonoos.

Timosthenes, Aiginetan, elder brother of Alkimedon.

Tiryns, city of the Argolid.

m Tityos, son of Earth.

m Tlapolemos, son of Herakles and Astydameia, first colonist of Rhodes.

Trident-lifter, Poseidon.

Tritonis, lake in north Africa.

Troy, city in north-west Asia Minor.

n Tyndaridai, Kastor and Polydeukes.
n Typhos, hundred-headed giant.
Tyrrhenians, Etruscans.

Vineland, Aigina.

Xanthos, river of south-west Asia Minor.
Xenarkes, Aiginetan, father of Aristomenes.
Xenokrates, brother of Theron and father of Thrasyboulos.
Xenophon, Korinthian, son of Thessalos.

INDEX